"Christ in Prophecy"

Study Guide

Dr. David R. Reagan

Estus + Lita
God bless you!
Maranatha!
Dave Reagan
2/07

LAMB
& LION
MINISTRIES

Dedicated to the memory of

Victor Broaddus

The remarkable Philippine missionary
who introduced me to Bible prophecy.

First Edition — August 1987
Second Edition — May 2001
Third Edition — November 2006

ISBN-13: 978-0-945593-16-4
ISBN-10: 0-945593-16-3
Library of Congress Control Number: 2006909320

All illustrations drawn by Jack Hamm.

Cover design by Richard Slaton.

The poem on page 6, "Epistle," by Carl Sandburg is taken from
Complete Poems by Carl Sandburg and is used by permission
of Harcourt Brace Jovanovich Publishing Company.

All scripture quotations are from the New American Standard Bible
Updated Edition © The Lockman Foundation, 1995.

**LAMB
& LION
MINISTRIES**

**P.O. Box 919, McKinney, TX 75070
972/736-3567 ✡ lamblion@lamblion.com
www.lamblion.com**

TABLE OF CONTENTS

Part One

The First Advent of Jesus in Bible Prophecy

Part Two

The Second Advent of Jesus in Old Testament Prophecy

Part Three

The Second Advent of Jesus in New Testament Prophecy

Part Four

Indexes of Prophecies

Books by
Dr. David R. Reagan

The Christ in Prophecy Study Guide
(Lamb & Lion Ministries, 1987, 2001, 2006)

Trusting God: Learning to Walk by Faith
(Huntington House, Inc., 1987. Second edition, 1994)

Jesus is Coming Again!
(Harvest House, 1992)

The Master Plan: Making Sense of the Controversies
Surrounding Bible Prophecy Today
(Harvest House, 1993)

Living for Christ in the End Times:
Balancing Today with the Hope of Tomorrow
(New Leaf Press, 2000)

Wrath & Glory: The Meaning of Revelation
(New Leaf Press, 2001)

America the Beautiful? The United States in Bible Prophecy
(Lamb & Lion Ministries, 2003. Second edition, 2006)

God's Plan for the Ages: The Blueprint of Bible Prophecy
(Lamb & Lion Ministries, 2005)

Video Programs featuring
Dr. David R. Reagan
(Partial listing)

Israel in Bible Prophecy
(Lamb & Lion Ministries, 1987. Second edition, 2001)

The Rapture Kit: A Multi-Media Study
(Lamb & Lion Ministries, 1997)

The Signs of the Times Kit: A Multi-Media Study
(Lamb & Lion Ministries, 1998)

Preaching Bible Prophecy
(Lamb & Lion Ministries, 2000)

A Pilgrimage to the Holy Land
(Lamb & Lion Ministries, 2000)

Revelation Revealed
(Lamb & Lion Ministries, 2003)

Jerusalem Through Spiritual Eyes
(Lamb & Lion Ministries, 2004)

The Galilee of Jesus
(Lamb & Lion Ministries, 2005)

Part One

THE FIRST ADVENT OF JESUS IN BIBLE PROPHECY

"... Behold, a virgin will be with child and bear a son, and she will call His name Immanuel [God with us]." — Isaiah 7:14

Epistle

Carl Sandburg

Jesus loved the sunsets on Galilee.

Jesus loved the fishing boats forming silhouettes against the sunsets on Galilee.

Jesus loved the fishermen on the fishing boats forming silhouettes against the sunsets on Galilee.

When Jesus said: "Goodby, goodby, I will come again . . ."

Jesus meant that goodby for the sunsets, the fishing boats, the fishermen, the silhouettes all and any against the sunsets of Galilee.

The goodby and the promise meant all or nothing.

A. FIRST ADVENT PROPHECIES IN THE OLD TESTAMENT

1. INTRODUCTION

Most scholars agree that there are about 300 prophecies in the Old Testament that relate to the First Coming of the Messiah. But, these are not 300 different prophecies. Many, like the prophecy that the Messiah will be born of the seed of Abraham, are repeated several times.

When all the repetitive prophecies are culled out, there remain slightly more than one hundred distinctively different, specific prophecies about the Messiah's First Advent. These prophecies are outlined in detail later in this chapter.

Prophetic Types

In addition to the specific prophecies, there are many prophecies in type which point to various aspects of the First Advent.

Prophecy in type is symbolic prophecy. Paul refers to this kind of prophecy in Romans 5:14 where he points to Adam as "a type of Him who was to come." The author of Hebrews also refers to it when he states that the High Priest and the Tabernacle were a "shadow of heavenly things" (Hebrews 8:5).

The Gospels relate that Jesus spent some of the 40 days between His resurrection and ascension teaching the Scriptures to His disciples. Luke says "He opened their minds to understand the Scriptures" (Luke 24:25). I suspect that much of His teaching focused on prophecy in type. He most likely went through the Torah, scroll by scroll, and showed them how to find Him in every column, hidden in prophetic types.

A good example is Boaz in the book of Ruth. He is a beautiful prophetic type of Jesus because he is a Kinsman-Redeemer who takes a Gentile bride. In like manner, Hosea and his tumultuous relationship with his prostitute wife pictures God's relationship with His unfaithful wife, Israel, and His willingness, in His perfect love, to pay the price of redemption to make it possible for His wife to be reconciled to Him. Nehemiah tells us that the Judges were "Saviors" (Nehemiah 9:27), and in that sense, they pointed to the ultimate Savior, the Messiah.

Joshua, Jeremiah, and Daniel all give us insights about the faith, courage, and compassion of the Messiah. Joshua and Jesus even had exactly the same name — Yeshua, meaning the Salvation of God. "Joshua" is an English transliteration of the Hebrew name, Yeshua, and "Jesus" is a transliteration of the same name from the Greek.

Jesus identified Jonah as a prophetic type. He pointed out that just as Jonah had been entombed three days in the belly of a great fish, He likewise would be entombed in the earth for three days (Matthew 12:38-40).

Abraham's experience in offering his son Isaac as a sacrifice is one of the foremost prophetic types in the Old Testament (Genesis 22). It is the picture of a loving father willing to sacrifice his innocent son. The event even took place on Mt. Moriah where Jesus would later be crucified. This event is specifically referred to in the New Testament as a prophetic type pointing symbolically to the death and resurrection of Jesus (Hebrews 11:19).

Prophetic Anti-Types

Another major Old Testament figure who serves as a type of Christ is Adam, although he is really more of an anti-type. An anti-type is a negative symbol that points to positive truths. Adam's anti-typical prophetic nature is illustrated below in Figure 1.

Satan is an anti-type of Christ. His weaknesses point to Jesus' strengths. For example, the basic sin that caused his fall was pride (Isaiah 14:13-14). By contrast, Jesus was the essence of humility (Philippians 2:5-8). Satan's agent in the Tribulation, the Antichrist, will also be an anti-type of the true Christ. Whereas the Antichrist will be a deceiver, a liar and a blasphemer (Revelation 13:1-6), Jesus Christ will return as the "Faithful and True" One (Revelation 19:11).

This is one of the themes of the book of Hebrews. Comparing the sacrifice of animals under the Law to the sacrifice of Jesus, the book of Hebrews says: "For if the blood of goats and bulls and the ashes of a heifer sprinkling those who have been defiled, sanctify for the cleansing of the flesh, how much more will the blood of Christ, who through the eternal Spirit offered Himself without blemish to God, cleanse your conscience from dead works to serve the living God?" (Hebrews 9:13-14).

One of the most detailed ceremonial

Figure 1
Adam as an Anti-type to Jesus

Adam	Jesus
1) A living soul. (1 Corinthians 15:45)	1) A life-giving spirit. (1 Corinthians 15:45)
2) Of the earth. (1 Corinthians 15:47)	2) From Heaven. (1 Corinthians 15:47)
3) Rebelled against God. (Genesis 3:1-7)	3) Obeyed God perfectly. (Hebrews 5:8-9)
4) Through him, all were made sinners. (Romans 5:19)	4) Through Him, many will be made righteous. (Romans 5:19)
5) Brought death. (Romans 5:14-15; 1 Corinthians 15:22)	5) Brought life. (Hebrews 2:14-15)
6) Lost dominion. (Genesis 1:26 and Genesis 3:17-24)	6) Won dominion. (Hebrews 2:5-9).

Ceremonial Types

Much of the ceremonial law in the Law of Moses is deeply steeped in symbolic typology related to the First Advent. All the various types of sin offerings (Leviticus 1-6) pointed the worshiper to the Messiah who would serve as the perfect and all-sufficient offering for all our sins.

types of the Messiah to be found in the Old Testament scriptures is the Tabernacle of Moses. Every aspect of the Tabernacle was prophetic of the Messiah. See Figure 2 on the next page.

Figure 2

The Tabernacle of Moses as a Prophetic Type

1) The Gate	— Jesus as the Door. (John 10:9)
2) The Altar	— Jesus as the Sacrificial Lamb. (John 1:29)
3) The Laver	— Jesus as the Spirit Baptizer. (John 1:33)
4) The Shewbread	— Jesus as the Bread of Life. (John 6:35)
5) The Candlestick	— Jesus as the Light of the World. (John 8:12)
6) The Incense	— Jesus as the Intercessor who offers the prayers of the Saints to God. (Hebrews 4:14-16)
7) The Veil	— Jesus as the one who would rend the veil, making it possible for the Saints to have direct access to God through Him. (Matthew 27:51)
8) The High Priest	— Jesus as our High Priest who enters the Holy of Holies in Heaven as our Mediator before the Father. (Hebrews 8:1-2 and Hebrews 9:24)

The Ark of the Covenant

The Holy of Holies contained the Ark of the Covenant. Everything about the Ark was symbolic of the Messiah. It was made of wood, indicating the Messiah would be a human. It was overlaid with gold, signifying the Messiah would be divine. It contained three objects — the tablets of stone, a pot of manna, and Aaron's rod that budded. The tablets signified that the Messiah would have the Law of God in His heart. The manna meant the Messiah would be the Bread of Life. The rod with blooms was a prophecy that the Messiah would arise from the dead.

The lid of the Ark was called the Mercy Seat. Once a year the High Priest sprinkled blood on the Mercy Seat to atone for the sins of Israel. The Mercy Seat pointed to the fact that through the work of the Messiah the mercy of God would cover the Law. The blood foreshadowed the fact that the Messiah would have to shed His own blood to atone for our sins.

Jesus fulfilled every prophetic type of the Ark. He was God in the flesh (John 10:30). He had the Law in His heart (Matthew 5:17). He declared Himself to be the "Bread of Life" (John 6:35). And He shed His blood on the Cross, atoning for our sins and covering the Law with Grace (Romans 3:21-26).

Historical Types

Even some historical events are prophetic types. A dramatic example is the Passover experience (Exodus 12). To prevent the death of the first born of both man and beast in each family on the day that the Lord passed over Egypt, each Jewish family had to slay a lamb and put its blood on the doorposts and lintels of their houses. This was a prophetic symbol that the salvation of all men would be made possible through the sacrifice of the Lamb of God and the appropriation of His blood.

Another historical event with prophetic significance occurred in the Wilderness when the Children of Israel were attacked by fiery serpents (Numbers 21:4-9). A bronze serpent was placed on a pole and lifted up for all to see. Those bitten by the snakes were told to look upon the bronze serpent for healing.

That bronze serpent was a type of Christ. Just as the Israelites bitten by the fiery serpents died, so men bitten by Satan's serpent of sin must suffer spiritual death. And just as the bronze serpent was lifted up for their salvation, in like manner, Jesus was lifted up on a pole to save men from their sins (John 3:14).

Bronze and serpents are both Biblical symbols of sin. Jesus is typified as a brazen serpent on a pole because He took the sins of Mankind upon Himself while He was on the Cross.

Finally, those bitten by the snakes only had to look in faith at the bronze serpent in order to be healed. And in like manner, sinners need only look to Jesus in faith in order to be saved.

The early history of the Jewish nation is the story of Jesus in prophetic type. The Children of Israel were born in Canaan, descended into Egypt, emerged through the Red Sea (the baptism of Moses), endured testing in the Wilderness, and then entered the Promised Land. Likewise, Jesus was born in Canaan, descended into Egypt, emerged publicly at His baptism, and led the way to Heaven.

Prophecy Outline

In the outline that follows, 109 of the Old Testament's specific prophecies about the First Advent are identified and classified into categories related to the chronology of the life of Christ. In each case the prophecy's origin is cited from a major Old Testament source (with alternative sources indicated in parentheses). Then, a New Testament source is quoted to show the prophecy's fulfillment in the life of Jesus. One interesting thing to note is that most of the 34 prophecies regarding the Messiah's death were all fulfilled in a 24 hour period.

The Gospel of Matthew was written to the Jews. For this reason, it emphasizes the fulfillment of Jewish prophecy in the life of Jesus. Matthew is, therefore, an excellent place to start in any study of prophecy concerning the First Advent. ✛

"The testimony of Jesus is the spirit of prophecy." — Revelation 19:10

2. OUTLINE OF FIRST ADVENT PROPHECIES IN THE OLD TESTAMENT

A. THE MESSIAH'S LINEAGE

Old Testament Source	Prophecy	New Testament Fulfillment
". . . Blessed be the Lord, the God of Shem, and let Canaan be his servant." — Genesis 9:26	1) From the Shemite branch of humanity	"[Jesus] . . . the son of Shem, the son of Noah . . ." — Luke 3:36
". . . and in you [Abraham] all the nations of the earth shall be blessed." — Genesis 12:3 (Genesis 18:18 and 22:18)	2) Through Abraham	"The record of the genealogy of of Jesus the Messiah, the son of David, the son of Abraham . . ." — Matthew 1:1 (Luke 3:34; Acts 3:25; and Galatians 3:16)
"My Covenant I will establish with Isaac, whom Sarah shall bear to you . . ." — Genesis 17:21 (Genesis 17:19 and 21:12)	3) Through Abraham's son, Isaac	"[Jesus] . . . the son of Isaac, the son of Abraham . . ." — Luke 3:34 (Matthew 1:2 and Romans 9:7)
". . . and in you [Jacob] and in your descendants shall all the families of the earth be blessed." — Genesis 28:14 (Genesis 27:28-29; 28:4; 35:9-12)	4) Through Isaac's son, Jacob	"[Jesus] . . . the son of Jacob, the son of Isaac . . ." — Luke 3:34 (Matthew 1:2 and Acts 7:8)
"Judah, your brothers shall praise you . . . Your father's sons shall bow down before you." — Genesis 49:8 (Genesis 49:10 and Micah 5:2)	5) Through the tribe of Judah	"[Jesus] . . . the son of Judah, the son of Jacob . . ." — Luke 3:33-34 (Matthew 1:2; Hebrews 7:14; and Revelation 5:5)

Old Testament Source	Prophecy	New Testament Fulfillment
"Then a shoot will spring from the stem of Jesse, and a branch from his roots will bear fruit." — Isaiah 11:1	**6) Through the family of Jesse**	"[Jesus] . . . the son of Jesse . . ." — Luke 3:32 (Matthew 1:6)
"'Behold, the days are coming,' declares the Lord, 'when I shall raise up for David a righteous Branch . . .'" — Jeremiah 23:5 (2 Samuel 7:12-14; Psalm 89:20, 28-39; and Psalm 132:10-12)	**7) Through the house of David**	"[Jesus] . . . the son of David, the son of Jesse . . ." — Luke 3:31-32 (Matthew 1:6; John 7:42; and Romans 1:3)

B. THE MESSIAH'S BIRTH AND CHILDHOOD

Old Testament Source	Prophecy	New Testament Fulfillment
"The scepter shall not depart from Judah . . . until Shiloh comes, and to him shall be the obedience of the peoples." — Genesis 49:10 (Note: The timing of the Lord's birth could also be calculated from Daniel 9:24-26. That passage says the Messiah will come on the scene 483 years after the issuance of a decree to rebuild Jerusalem.)	**1) Timing of the birth**	Approximately 7 A.D. the Romans abolished the power of the Sanhedrin Council in Judah to pronounce the death penalty — thus the scepter (power) passed from Judah. Jesus had been born in 4 B.C., during the reign of Herod (Matthew 2:1), so Shiloh (the Messiah) had come shortly before the scepter departed — just as prophesied.
"But as for you, Bethlehem Ephrathah, too little to be among the clans of Judah, from you One will go forth for Me to be ruler in Israel." — Micah 5:2 (Note: The term "Ephrathah" refers to the area south of Jerusalem, in order to differentiate this Bethlehem from the one located at that time in the north, in the Galilee area.)	**2) Place of the birth**	"Now after Jesus was born in Bethlehem of Judea in the days of Herod the king . . ." — Matthew 2:1 (Luke 2:1-7 and John 7:42)

Old Testament Source	Prophecy	New Testament Fulfillment
"For a child will be born to us, a son will be given to us . . ." — Isaiah 9:6	**3) Born in the flesh**	". . . for today in the city of David there has been born for you a Savior, who is Christ the Lord." — Luke 2:11
"A star shall come forth from Jacob, And a scepter shall rise from Israel." Numbers 24:17	**4) A star will signal the birth**	"We saw His star in the east, and have come to worship Him." — Matthew 2:2
". . . Behold, a virgin will be with child and bear a son, and she will call His name Immanuel." — Isaiah 7:14 (Genesis 3:15 and Jeremiah 31:22)	**5) Born of a virgin**	"Mary said to the angel, 'How can this be, since I am a virgin?' The angel answered and said to her, 'The Holy Spirit will come upon you, and the power of the Most High will overshadow you . . .'" — Luke 1:34-35 (Matthew 1:18; Galatians 4:4; and Revelation 12:5)
". . . and she will call His name Immanuel." [Meaning "God is with us."] — Isaiah 7:14	**6) Divine name**	". . . you shall call His name Jesus [God's Salvation], for He will save His people from their sins." — Matthew 1:21
"Let the kings of Tarshish and of the islands bring presents; the kings of Sheba and Seba offer gifts. And let all kings bow down before Him . . ." — Psalm 72:10-11	**7) Presented with gifts at birth**	". . . magi from the east arrived . . . [and] after coming into the house they saw the Child . . . and they fell to the ground and worshiped Him. Then, opening their treasures, they presented to Him gifts of gold, frankincense, and myrrh." — Matthew 2:1, 11
"Thus says the Lord, 'A voice is heard in Ramah, lamentation and bitter weeping. Rachel is weeping for her children; she refuses to be comforted for her children, because they are no more.'" — Jeremiah 31:15	**8) Infants massacred**	"Then when Herod saw that he had been tricked by the magi, he became very enraged, and sent and slew all the male children who were in Bethlehem and in all its vicinity, from two years old and under . . ." — Matthew 2:16

Old Testament Source	Prophecy	New Testament Fulfillment
"When Israel was a youth I loved him, and out of Egypt I called My son." — Hosea 11:1	**9) Sojourn in Egypt**	"So Joseph got up and took the Child and His mother while it was still night, and left for Egypt. He remained there until the death of Herod. This was to fulfill what had been spoken by the Lord through the prophet: 'Out of Egypt I called My Son.'" — Matthew 2:14-15
Matthew's reference (2:23) is uncertain. Some scholars believe it is derived from Isaiah 53:4 where the Messiah is referred to as a "pain bearer." The word for pain here is "natzri." Other scholars say Matthew is referring to Isaiah 11:1 where the Messiah is referred to as a "neser" — that is, a "branch" of Jesse.	**10) Reside in Nazareth**	"[Joseph] came and lived in a city called Nazareth. This was to fulfill what was spoken through the prophets: 'He shall be called a Nazarene.'" — Matthew 2:23
". . . He grew up before Him like a tender shoot, and like a root out of parched ground . . ." — Isaiah 53:2	**11) Grow up in poverty**	"Is not this [Jesus] the carpenter, the son of Mary, and brother of James and Joses and Judas and Simon?"— Mark 6:3 (Luke 9:58) "And Jesus said to him, 'The foxes have holes and the birds of the air have nests, but the Son of Man has nowhere to lay His head.'" — Luke 9:58
"The Spirit of the Lord will rest on Him, the spirit of wisdom and understanding. The spirit of counsel and strength, the spirit of knowledge and the fear of the Lord." — Isaiah 11:1-2	**12) Spirit-filled and anointed from birth**	"They found Him in the temple [at age 12] sitting in the midst of teachers, both listening to them and asking them questions. And all who heard Him were amazed at His understanding and His answers." — Luke 2:46-47

C. THE MESSIAH'S LIFE AND MINISTRY

Old Testament Source	Prophecy	New Testament Fulfillment
"A voice is calling, 'Clear the way for the Lord in the wilderness; make smooth in the desert a highway for our God.'" — Isaiah 40.3 (Malachi 3:1)	1) **Preceded by a prophet who would prepare His way**	"Now in those days John the Baptist came, preaching in the wilderness of Judea, saying, 'Repent, for the kingdom of heaven is at hand.' For this is the one referred to by Isaiah the prophet . . ." — Matthew 3:1-3 (Matthew 11:7-14)
"Behold, My Servant, whom I uphold; My chosen one in whom My soul delights. I have put My Spirit upon Him . . ." — Isaiah 42:1 (Isaiah 11:2)	2) **Receive a special anointing by the Spirit**	". . . and the Holy Spirit descended upon Him [Jesus] in bodily form like a dove, and a voice came out of heaven, 'You are My beloved Son . . .'" — Luke 3:22
"And I will put enmity between you [Satan] and the woman, and between your seed and her seed; He shall bruise you [Satan] on the head, and you shall bruise Him [the Messiah] on the heel." — Genesis 3:15	3) **Do battle with Satan**	"Then Jesus was led up by the Spirit into the wilderness to be tempted by the devil." — Matthew 4:1 (Matthew 4:1-11)
"For He will give His angels charge concerning you, to guard you in all your ways." — Psalm 91:11	4) **Receive the ministry of angels**	"Then the devil left Him; and behold, angels came and began to minister to Him." — Matthew 4:11 (Matthew 26:53 and Luke 22:43)
". . . in earlier times He treated the land of Zebulun and the land of Naphtali with contempt, but later on He shall make it glorious, by way of the sea, on the other side of Jordan, Galilee of the Gentiles." — Isaiah 9:1	5) **Ministry centered in Galilee**	". . . and leaving Nazareth, He [Jesus] came and settled in Capernaum which is by the sea, in the region of Zebulun and Naphtali." — Matthew 4:13 (Matthew 4:12-16)

Old Testament Source	Prophecy	New Testament Fulfillment
"He [the Servant] will not cry out or raise His voice, nor make His voice heard in the street." — Isaiah 42:2	6) Unpretentious ministry	"So, Jesus, perceiving that they were intending to come and take Him by force to make Him king, withdrew again to the mountain by Himself alone." — John 6:15
". . . He [the Messiah] has no stately form or majesty that we should look upon Him, nor appearance that we should be attracted to Him." — Isaiah 53:2	7) Power of ministry not based on personal appearance	"When Jesus had finished these words, the crowds were amazed at His teaching; for He was teaching them as one having authority, and not as their scribes." — Matthew 7:28-29
"I have proclaimed glad tidings of righteousness in the great congregation; behold, I will not restrain my lips . . ." — Psalm 40:9 (Isaiah 61:1)	8) Preacher	"From that time Jesus began to preach and say, 'Repent, for the kingdom of heaven is at hand.'" — Matthew 4:17 (Luke 8:1)
"I will open my mouth in a parable; I will utter dark sayings of old." — Psalm 78:2 "Go and tell this people: 'Keep on listening, but do not perceive; keep on looking, but do not understand.'" — Isaiah 6:9	9) Teacher in parables	"All these things Jesus spoke to the crowds in parables, and He did not speak to them without a parable. This was to fulfill what was spoken through the prophet . . ." — Matthew 13:34-35 (Matthew 13:10-16)
"'I [the Lord] will raise up a prophet from among their countrymen like you [Moses], and I will put My words in his mouth, and he shall speak to them all that I command him.'" — Deuteronomy 18:15, 18	10) Prophet	"And the crowds were saying, 'This is the prophet Jesus, from Nazareth in Galilee.'" — Matthew 21:11 (Matthew 21:46 and John 5:46)

Old Testament Source	Prophecy	New Testament Fulfillment
"The Lord is our judge . . . He will save us." — Isaiah 33:22	**11) Judge**	"As I hear, I judge; and My judgment is just, because I do not seek My own will, but the will of Him who sent Me." — John 5:30 (John 5:22 and John 8:16)
"And the Spirit of the Lord will rest on Him . . . the spirit of . . . strength . . ." — Isaiah 11:2	**12) Miracle worker**	". . . this man [Nicodemus] came to Jesus by night and said to Him, 'Rabbi, we know that You have come from God as a teacher; for no one can do these signs that You do unless God is with him.'" — John 3:2 (John 2:11, 23; John 11:47; and John 12:37)
"In return for my love they act as my accusers; but I am in prayer." — Psalm 109:4	**13) Man of prayer**	"Now He was telling them a parable to show that at all times they ought to pray and not lose heart . . ." — Luke 18:1 (Matthew 6:9-13; Luke 11:1-4; and Hebrews 7:25)
"You [God] made me trust when upon my mother's breasts. Upon You I was cast from birth; You have been my God from my mother's womb." — Psalm 22:9-10	**14) A Man whose reliance and trust is in God**	"Truly, truly, I say to you, the Son can do nothing of Himself, unless it is something He sees the Father doing; for whatever the Father does, these things the Son also does in like manner." — John 5:19 (John 10:37-38; John 12:49; and John 14:10)
"I delight to do Your will, O my God; Your law is within my heart." — Psalm 40:8	**15) A Man of obedience**	"Jesus said to them, 'My food is to do the will of Him who sent Me and to accomplish His work.'" — John 4:34 (Matthew 5:17 and Hebrews 5:8-9)

Old Testament Source	Prophecy	New Testament Fulfillment
"The Spirit of the Lord will rest on Him, the spirit of wisdom and understanding . . . the spirit of knowledge and the fear of the Lord." man — Isaiah 11:2	**16) A Man of wisdom, understanding and knowledge**	"He came to His hometown and began teaching them in their synagogue, so that they became astonished, and said, 'Where did this get this wisdom, and these miraculous powers?'" — Matthew 13:54 (Matthew 7:28 and Luke 2:47)
"And the Spirit of the Lord will rest on Him . . . the spirit of counsel . . ." Isaiah 11:2	**17) A Man of counsel**	"Now there was a man of the Pharisees, named Nicodemus, a ruler of the Jews; this man came to Jesus by night, and said to Him . . . 'How can a man be born when he is old?'" — John 3:1, 4 "[The Samaritan woman] said to Him, 'Sir, You have nothing to draw with and the well is deep; where then do You get that living water?'" — John 4:11 (Luke 12:13-21 and Luke 18:18-27)
"Behold, your king is coming to you; He is just and endowed with salvation, humble, and mounted on a donkey . . ." — Zechariah 9:9 (Micah 5:2)	**18) Humble in spirit**	". . . He humbled Himself by becoming obedient to the point of death . . ." — Philippians 2:8 (Matthew 5:5; Matthew 11:29; Matthew 18:4 and Mark 10:43-45)
"The Lord is gracious and merciful; slow to anger and great in loving-kindness." — Psalm 145:8 (Psalm 86:15 and Isaiah 53:7)	**19) Patient**	". . . I found mercy, so that in me [Paul] as the foremost [sinner], Jesus Christ might demonstrate His perfect patience . . ." — 1 Timothy 1:16 (Matthew 5:39-42 and 2 Peter 3:9)

Old Testament Source	Prophecy	New Testament Fulfillment
"... the lovingkindness of the Lord is from everlasting to everlasting on those who fear Him." — Psalm 103:17 (Psalm 89:14 and Isaiah 53)	20) Loving and merciful	"Greater love has no one than this, that one lay down his life for his friends." — John 15:13 (Matthew 5:43-44; John 13:34-35; and John 15:12-13)
"... zeal for Your house has consumed me ..." — Psalm 69:9 (Malachi 3:1-4)	21) Zeal for God's House in Jerusalem	"And He found in the temple those who were selling ... And He made a scourge of cords, and drove them all out of the temple ... His disciples remembered what was written, 'Zeal for Your house will consume me.'" — John 2:14-16 (Mark 11:15-18 and Luke 19:45-46)
"The Spirit of the Lord God is upon me ... to proclaim the favorable year of the Lord." — Isaiah 61:1-2	22) Proclaim a Jubilee Note: Jesus began His ministry in 27 A.D. — the last year of Jubilee before the Jews went into captivity.	"And the book of the prophet Isaiah was handed to Him. And He opened the book and found the place where it was written, 'The Spirit of the Lord is upon me ...' And He began to say to them, 'Today this Scripture has been fulfilled in your hearing.'" — Luke 4:17, 18, 21
"The Spirit of the Lord is upon me, because the Lord has anointed me to bring good news to the afflicted ..." — Isaiah 61:1	23) Preach the Gospel to the poor	"Jesus answered and said to them, 'Go and report to John what you hear and see: ... the poor have the gospel preached to them.'" — Matthew 11:4-5 (Matthew 5, 6, and 7)
"The Spirit of the Lord is upon me, because the Lord has anointed me ... to bind up the broken-hearted ..." — Isaiah 61:1	24) Comfort the broken-hearted	"Come to Me, all who are weary and heavy-laden, and I will give you rest." — Matthew 11:28 (Matthew 5:4 and John 16:20)

Old Testament Source	Prophecy	New Testament Fulfillment
"The Spirit of the Lord is upon me, because the Lord has anointed me . . . to proclaim liberty to captives, and freedom to prisoners." — Isaiah 61:1	**25) Proclaim liberty to captives**	". . . they brought to Him many who were demon-possessed; and He cast out the spirits with a word . . ." — Matthew 8:16 (Mark 1:32-34 and Luke 6:17-18)
"A bruised reed He will not break, and a dimly burning wick He will not extinguish." — Isaiah 42:3	**26) Minister to broken lives**	"The Pharisees . . . began grumbling . . . saying, 'Why do you eat and drink with the tax gatherers and sinners?' And Jesus answered . . . 'It is not those who are well who need a physician, but those who are sick.'" — Luke 5:30-31 (Matthew 9:10-13)
"Surely our griefs [sickness] He Himself bore, and our sorrows [pains] He carried . . . and by His scourging we are healed." — Isaiah 53:4-5	**27) Heal the sick**	". . . He cast out the spirits with a word, and healed all who were ill. This was to fulfill what was spoken through Isaiah the prophet: 'He Himself took our infirmities, and carried away our diseases.'" — Matthew 8:16-17 (Matthew 12:15-21)
"Then the eyes of the blind will be opened, and the ears of the deaf will be unstopped. Then the lame will leap like a deer, and the tongue of the mute will shout for joy." — Isaiah 35:5-6	**28) Heal those with special afflictions** Note: The context of the Isaiah passage makes it clear that its ultimate fulfillment will occur during the Millennium. But Jesus makes it clear that it was pre-filled in His healing ministry.	"Jesus answered . . . 'Go and report to John what you hear and see: the blind receive sight and the lame walk, the lepers are cleansed and the deaf hear, and the dead are raised up . . .'" — Matthew 11:4-5 (Matthew 4:24; Matthew 8:1-4; Mark 10:46-52; John 5:1-9; and John 11:40-44)

Old Testament Source	Prophecy	New Testament Fulfillment
"Those who hate me without a cause are more than the hairs of my head . . ." — Psalm 69:4	**29) Hated without cause**	". . . now they have both seen and hated Me and My Father as well. But they have done this in order to fulfill the word that is written in their Law, 'They hated Me without a cause.'" — John 15:24-25
"Because for Your sake I have borne reproach; dishonor has covered my face. I have become estranged from my brothers, and an alien to my mother's sons." — Psalm 69:7-8 (Psalm 118:22 and Isaiah 49:7; and Isaiah 53:3)	**30) Despised and rejected by His own people, the Jews**	"He came to His own, and those who were His own did not receive Him." — John 1:11 (Matthew 21:33-46 and John 7:5, 48)
". . . this people draw near with their words and honor Me with their lip service, but they remove their hearts far from Me, and their reverence for Me consists of tradition learned by rote." — Isaiah 29:13	**31) Rejected by the Jews because they would honor tradition more than God's Word**	"And He said to them, 'Rightly did Isaiah prophesy of you hypocrites . . . Neglecting the commandment of God, you hold to the tradition of men.'" — Mark 7:6, 8 (Matthew 15:1-9)
"From the mouth of infants and nursing babes You have established strength . . ." — Psalm 8:2	**32) Praised by babes and infants**	". . . when the chief priests and the scribes saw . . . the children . . . shouting . . . 'Hosanna to the Son of David,' they became indignant, and said to Him, 'Do You hear what these children are saying?' And Jesus said to them, 'Yes; have you never read [the prophecy]?'" — Matthew 21:15-16
". . . I will also make You a light of the nations so that My salvation may reach to the end of the earth." — Isaiah 49:6 (Isaiah 42:1-4)	**33) Offered to the Gentiles**	"But as many as received Him, to them He gave the right to become children of God . . ." — John 1:12 (Acts 10 and Romans 1:16)

Old Testament Source	Prophecy	New Testament Fulfillment
"I will also have compassion on her who had not obtained compassion, and I will say to those who were not My people, 'You are my people!' And they will say, 'You are my God!'" — Hosea 2:23	**34) Accepted by the Gentiles**	"Therefore, let it be known to you that this salvation of God has been sent to the Gentiles; they will also listen." — Acts 28:28 (Acts 13:44-48)

D. THE MESSIAH'S NATURE

Old Testament Source	Prophecy	New Testament Fulfillment
"But as for you, Bethlehem . . . from you One will go forth for Me to be ruler in Israel. His goings forth are from long ago, from the days of eternity." — Micah 5:2	**1) Eternal**	"In the beginning was the Word, and the Word was with God, and the Word was God . . . And the Word became flesh, and dwelt among us . . ." — John 1:1, 14 (Colossians 1:17; Hebrews 1:2, 8; and Revelation 22:13)
"For a child will be born to us . . . and His name will be called Wonderful Counselor, Mighty God, Eternal Father, Prince of Peace." — Isaiah 9:6 (Isaiah 7:14)	**2) Divine**	"I and the Father are one." — John 10:30 (Matthew 1:22-23; John 20:28; Philippians 2:6; Colossians 1:15, 19; and Hebrews 1:3)
". . . You have made him [the son of man] a little lower than God, and You crown him with glory and majesty!" — Psalm 8:5 (Daniel 7:13)	**3) Human**	"And the Word became flesh, and dwelt among us, and we saw His glory, glory as of the only begotten from the Father . . ." — John 1:14 (Philippians 2:5-8 and Hebrews 2:5-9)
". . . He said to me, 'You are My Son, today I have begotten You.'" — Psalm 2:7 (Psalm 89:26-27 and 2 Samuel 7:14)	**4) Son of God**	". . . and behold, a voice out of the heavens, said, 'This is My beloved Son, in whom I am well-pleased.'" — Matthew 3:17 (Matthew 17:5 and John 3:16)

Old Testament Source	Prophecy	New Testament Fulfillment
"I kept looking in the night visions, and behold, with the clouds of heaven One like a Son of Man was coming, and He came up to the Ancient of Days . . ." — Daniel 7:13	**5) Son of Man**	"Jesus said to him, 'The foxes have holes and the birds of the air have nests, but the Son of Man has nowhere to lay His head.'" — Matthew 8:20 (Mark 2:10; Luke 12:10; and John 6:27)
"The kings of the earth take their stand and the rulers take counsel together against the Lord and against His Anointed [the Messiah] . . ." — Psalm 2:2 (Psalm 45:7)	**6) Messiah — the Anointed One, the Christ**	". . . the angel said to them . . . 'Today in the city of David there has been born for you a Savior, who is Christ [Messiah] the Lord,'" — Luke 2:10-11 (Matthew 16:16 and Acts 2:36)
"The Lord says to my Lord: 'Sit at My right hand until I make Your enemies a footstool for Your feet.'" — Psalm 110:1	**7) Lord**	"You call Me [Jesus] Teacher and Lord; and you are right, for so I am." — John 13:13 (Luke 2:11; John 20:28, and Acts 2:36)
"The Spirit of the Lord will rest on Him . . . the spirit of . . . the fear of the Lord. And He will delight in the fear of the Lord . . ." — Isaiah 11:2-3	**8) God Centered**	"I glorified You on the earth, having accomplished the work which You have given Me to do . . . I have manifested Your name to the men whom You gave Me out of the world . . ." — John 17:4, 6 (John 12:49; John 14:10; and John 15:23)
". . . the holy God will show Himself holy in righteousness." — Isaiah 5:16 (Isaiah 6:3 and Isaiah 8:13)	**9) Holy**	"We [Peter and the disciples] have come to know that You [Jesus] are the Holy One of God." — John 6:69 (Mark 1:24; Luke 1:35; and Acts 3:14)

Old Testament Source	Prophecy	New Testament Fulfillment
". . . by His knowledge the Righteous One, My Servant, will justify the many . . ." — Isaiah 53:11 (Psalm 45:7)	10) Righteous	"Which one of the prophets did your fathers not persecute? And they killed those who had previously announced the coming of the Righteous One, whose betrayers and murderers you have now become . . ." — Acts 7:52 (Acts 3:14; 22:14; 1 Corinthians 1:30; Hebrews 1:8-9; and 1 John 2:1)
". . . to all generations I will make known Your faithfulness with my mouth . . . In the heavens You will establish Your faithfulness." — Psalm 89:1-2 (Psalm 40:10; Psalm 57:10; and Psalm 117:2)	11) Faithful and True Witness	"To the angel of the church in Laodicea write: The Amen, the faithful and true Witness [Jesus] . . . says: . . ." — Revelation 3:14 (Revelation 1:5 and Revelation 19:11)
"Behold, My Servant, whom I uphold, My chosen one in whom My soul delights." — Isaiah 42:1 (Isaiah 49:7 and Zechariah 3:8)	12) Servant of God	". . . although He existed in the form of God, [Jesus] did not regard equality with God a thing to be grasped, but emptied Himself, taking the form of a bond-servant . . ." — Philippians 2:6-7 (Matthew 20:26-28)
"The Lord is my shepherd, I shall not want." — Psalm 23:1 (Psalm 23:1-6; Isaiah 40:11; and Zechariah 11:4-14)	13) A Loving Shepherd	" I am the good shepherd; the good shepherd lays down His life for the sheep." — John 10:11 (John 10:1-18; Hebrews 13:20; and 1 Peter 5:4)
". . . like a lamb that is led to slaughter, and like a sheep that is silent before its shearers, so He did not open His mouth." — Isaiah 53:7	14) A Sacrificial Lamb	"The next day he [John the Baptist] saw Jesus coming to him and said, 'Behold, the lamb of God who takes away the sin of the world!'" — John 1:29 (John 1:36; 1 Peter 1:18-19; and Revelation 5:6, 12-13)

Old Testament Source	Prophecy	New Testament Fulfillment
"Surely our griefs He Himself bore, and our sorrows He carried . . . He was pierced through for our transgressions, He was crushed for our iniquities . . . The Lord has caused the iniquity of us all to fall on Him." — Isaiah 53:4-6	15) A Sin Bearer	". . . He Himself bore our sins in His body on the cross, so that we might die to sin and live to right-eousness; for by His wounds you were healed." — 1 Peter 2:24 (1 Corinthians 15:3; 2 Corinthians 5:21; and Hebrews 9:28)
"But the Lord was pleased to crush Him, putting Him to grief, if He would render Himself as a guilt offering . . ." — Isaiah 53:10	16) A Guilt Offering	"For if the blood of bulls and the ashes of a heifer . . . sanctify for the cleansing of the flesh, how much more will the blood of Christ, who through the eternal Spirit offered Himself without blemish to God, cleanse your conscience from dead works to serve the living God?" — Hebrews 9:13-14 (Romans 5:8-9; Ephesians 1:7; and 1 John 1:7)
"I am the Lord, I have called you in righteousness . . . and I will appoint you as a covenant to the people . . ." — Isaiah 42:6 (Isaiah 49:8)	17) Embodiment of God's Redemptive Covenant	"And in the same way He took the cup after they had eaten, saying 'This cup which is poured out for you is the new covenant in My blood.'" — Luke 22:20 (1 Corinthians 11:25 and Hebrews 8:6-13; and Hebrews 9:15-22)

E. THE MESSIAH'S DEATH

Old Testament Source	Prophecy	New Testament Fulfillment
"So you are to know and discern that from the issuing of a decree to restore and rebuild Jerusalem until Messiah the Prince there will be seven weeks and sixty-two weeks . . . Then after the sixty-two weeks the Messiah will be cut off . . ." — Daniel 9:25-26	**1) Timing of death**	The "weeks" in this prophecy refer to weeks of years. Thus, the Messiah will die 69 weeks of years (483 years) after the edict is issued to rebuild Jerusalem. The edict was issued in 445 BC by Artaxerxes. 483 years later, Jesus began His ministry (27 A.D.), leading to His being crucified ("cut off").
"Rejoice greatly, O daughter of Zion! Shout in triumph, O daughter of Jerusalem! Behold, your king is coming to you; He is just and endowed with salvation, humble, and mounted on a donkey . . ." Zechariah 9:9	**2) Entry into Jerusalem on a donkey**	". . . the large crowd . . . when they heard that Jesus was coming to Jerusalem, took the branches of the palm trees and went out to meet Him, and began to shout, 'Hosanna! Blessed is He who comes in the name of the Lord, even the King of Israel.' Jesus, finding a young donkey, sat on it; as it is written . . . 'Your King is coming, seated on a donkey's colt.'" — John 12:12-15 (Matthew 21:1-11 and Mark 11:1-10)
"He was despised and forsaken of men, a man of sorrows, and acquainted with grief . . . As a result of the anguish of His soul, He will see light and be satisfied." — Isaiah 53:3, 11 (Psalm 55:12-14)	**3) Experience profound grief and agony**	"And He took with Him Peter and the two sons of Zebedee, and began to be grieved and distressed. Then He said to them, 'My soul is deeply grieved, to the point of death . . .'" — Matthew 26:37-38 (Mark 14:32-42 and Luke 22:39-46)

Old Testament Source	Prophecy	New Testament Fulfillment
"Even my close friend, in whom I trusted, who ate my bread, has lifted up his heel against me." — Psalm 41:9	**4) Betrayal by a friend who would eat with Him**	". . . Jesus was reclining at the table with the twelve disciples. As they were eating, He said, 'Truly I say to you that one of You will betray Me.'" — Matthew 26:20-21 ". . . Judas, one of the twelve, came up. . . to Jesus and said, 'Hail, Rabbi!' and kissed Him." — Matthew 26:47, 49
"I said to them, 'If it is good in your sight, give me my wages; but if not, never mind!' So they weighed out thirty shekels of silver as my wages." — Zechariah 11:12	**5) Betrayal for 30 pieces of silver**	"Then one of the twelve, named Judas Iscariot, went to the chief priests, and said, 'What are you willing to give me to betray Him up to you?' And they weighed out thirty pieces of silver to him." — Matthew 26:14-15
"Then the Lord said to me, 'Throw it to the potter' . . . So I took the thirty shekels of silver and threw them to the potter in the house of the Lord." — Zechariah 11:13	**6) Disposition of the betrayal money**	". . . [Judas] felt remorse and returned the thirty pieces of silver to the chief priests and elders . . . And he threw the pieces of silver into the sanctuary and departed . . . The chief priests took . . . the pieces of silver [and] bought the Potter's Field as a burial place for strangers." — Matthew 27:3, 5-7
"Strike the Shepherd that the sheep may be scattered . . ." — Zechariah 13:7	**7) Forsaken by His disciples**	". . . Jesus said to the crowds, 'Have you come out with swords and clubs to arrest Me as you would against a robber?' . . . Then all the disciples left Him and fled." — Matthew 26:55-56
"Malicious witnesses rise up; they ask me of things that I do not know. They repay me evil for good, to the bereavement of my soul." — Psalm 35:11-12	**8) Accused by false witnesses**	"Now the chief priests and the whole Council kept trying to obtain false testimony against Jesus, so that they might put Him to death." — Matthew 26:59-63 (Mark 14:55-59)

Old Testament Source	Prophecy	New Testament Fulfillment
"He was oppressed and He was afflicted, yet He did not open His mouth . . ." — Isaiah 53:7	**9) Silent before His accusers**	". . . [Jesus] did not answer him [Pilate] with regard to even a single charge, so that the governor was quite amazed." — Matthew 27:14 (1 Peter 2:23)
". . . I did not cover My face from humiliation and spitting." — Isaiah 50:6	**10) Spat upon**	"Then they spat in His face . . ." — Matthew 26:67
". . . with a rod they will smite the judge of Israel on the cheek." — Micah 5:1	**11) Stricken**	"[They] beat Him with their fists; and others slapped Him." — Matthew 26:67
"I gave My back to those who strike Me . . ." — Isaiah 50:6	**12) Scourged**	". . . after having Jesus scourged, he [Pilate] handed Him over to be crucified." — Matthew 27:26
". . . His appearance was marred more than any man and His form more than the sons of men." — Isaiah 52:14	**13) Face beaten to a pulp**	"[The soldiers] took the reed and began to beat Him on the head." — Matthew 27:30
"[I gave] My cheeks to those who pluck out the beard . . ." — Isaiah 50:6	**14) Beard plucked**	There is no recorded fulfillment of Jesus' beard being plucked. It is likely one of the tortures He endured at the hands of the soldiers. (Mark 15:16-20)
"I did not cover My face from humiliation . . ." — Isaiah 50:6 (Psalm 69:19 and Psalm 22:6-18)	**15) Humiliated**	"[The soldiers] dressed Him up in purple, and after weaving a crown of thorns, they put it on Him; and they began to acclaim Him, 'Hail, King of the Jews!' They kept . . . kneeling and bowing before Him." — Mark 15:17-19

Old Testament Source	Prophecy	New Testament Fulfillment
"My strength is dried up like a potsherd . . ." — Psalm 22:15 (Psalm 109:22-25)	**16) Physical exhaustion**	"When they led Him away, they seized a man, Simon of Cyrene, coming in from the country, and placed on him the cross to carry behind Jesus." — Luke 23:26
". . . they pierced My hands and My feet." — Psalm 22:16 (Zechariah 13:6) Note: This prophecy was written by David 1,000 years before Jesus was born and 700 years before the Romans refined crucifixion as a method of execution.	**17) Crucified**	"When they came to the place called The Skull, there they crucified Him and the criminals, one on the right and the other on the left." — Luke 23:33
". . . He poured out Himself to death, and was numbered with the transgressors . . ." — Isaiah 53:12	**18) Identified with sinners**	"They crucified two robbers with Him, one on His right and one on His left." — Mark 15:27
". . . I am a worm and not a man, a reproach of men and despised by the people. All who see me sneer at me; they separate with the lip, they wag the head, saying, 'Commit yourself to the Lord; let Him deliver him . . . because He delights in him.'" — Psalm 22:6-8 (Psalm 69:20 and Psalm 109:25)	**19) Object of scorn and ridicule**	"And even the rulers were sneering at Him, saying, 'He saved others; let Him save Himself if this is the Christ of God, His Chosen One.' The soldiers mocked Him . . . [and] one of the criminals who were hanged there was hurling abuse at Him, saying, 'Are you not the Christ? Save Yourself and us!'" — Luke 23:35-36, 39
". . . my tongue cleaves to my jaws . . ." — Psalm 22:15 (Psalm 69:3, 21)	**20) Experience thirst**	". . . Jesus, knowing that all things had already been accomplished, to fulfill the Scripture, said, 'I am thirsty.'" — John 19:28

Old Testament Source	Prophecy	New Testament Fulfillment
"They also gave me gall for my food, and for my thirst they gave me vinegar to drink." — Psalm 69:21	**21) Given vinegar to drink**	". . . one of them ran, and taking a sponge, he filled it with sour wine and put it on a reed, and gave Him a drink." — Matthew 27:48
"My loved ones and my friends stand aloof from my plague; and my kinsmen stand afar off." — Psalm 38:11	**22) Friends stand far away**	"And all His acquaintances and the women who accompanied Him from Galilee were standing at a distance, seeing these things." — Luke 23:49
"They look, they stare at me . . ." — Psalm 22:17	**23) Stared at**	"And the people stood by, looking on." — Luke 23:35
"They divide my garments among them . . ." — Psalm 22:18	**24) Clothing divided among persecutors**	"Then the soldiers . . . took His outer garments and made four parts, a part to every soldier . . ." — John 19:23
". . . and for my clothing they cast lots." — Psalm 22:18	**25) Lots cast for robe**	". . . now the tunic was seamless, woven in one piece. So they said to one another, 'Let us not tear it, but cast lots for it to decide whose it shall be . . .'" — John 19:23-24
"'It will come about in that day,' declares the Lord God, 'that I shall make the sun go down at noon and make the earth dark in broad daylight.'" — Amos 8:9	**26) Darkness at noon**	"Now from the sixth hour [noon] darkness fell upon all the land until the ninth hour [3pm]." — Matthew 27:45
"My God, my God, why have You forsaken me?" — Psalm 22:1	**27) A cry of disorientation due to separation from God**	"About the ninth hour Jesus cried out with a loud voice, saying, . . . 'My God, My God, why have You forsaken Me?'" — Matthew 27:46

Old Testament Source	Prophecy	New Testament Fulfillment
"In return for my love they act as my accusers; but I am in prayer." — Psalm 109:4 (Isaiah 53:12)	**28) Pray for persecutors**	". . . Jesus was saying, 'Father, forgive them; for they do not know what they are doing.'" — Luke 23:34
"They will come and will declare His righteousness to a people who will be born, that He has performed it." — Psalm 22:31 Note: the phrase translated, "He has performed it," literally means, "He has finished it."	**29) A cry of victory**	"Therefore when Jesus had received the sour wine, He said, 'It is finished!' And He bowed His head and gave up His spirit." — John 19:30
"Into Your hand I commit my spirit; You have ransomed me, O Lord, God of truth." — Psalm 31:5	**30) Voluntary release of spirit spirit**	"And Jesus, crying out with a loud voice, said, 'Father, into Your hands I commit My spirit.' Having said this, He breathed His last." — Luke 23:46
"He keeps all his bones, not one of them is broken." — Psalm 34:20	**31) No bones broken**	"So the soldiers came, and broke the legs of the first man and of the other who was crucified with Him; but coming to Jesus, when they saw that He was already dead, they did not break His legs." — John 19:32-33
". . . they will look on Me whom they have pierced . . ." — Zechariah 12:10	**32) Pierced in the side**	"But one of the soldiers pierced His side with a spear . . ." — John 19:34
". . . my heart is like wax; it is melted within me." — Psalm 22:14	**33) Death by a broken heart**	"But one of the soldiers pierced His side with a spear, and immediately blood and water came out." — John 19:34 Note: The separation of the blood and water is a sign of a ruptured heart.

Old Testament Source	Prophecy	New Testament Fulfillment
"His grave was assigned with wicked men, yet He was with a rich man in His death . . ." — Isaiah 53:9	**34) Buried in a rich man's grave**	"When it was evening, there came a rich man from Arimathea, named Joseph . . . This man went to Pilate and asked for the body of Jesus . . . And Joseph took the body . . . and laid it in his own new tomb, which he had hewn out in the rock . . ." — Matthew 27:57-60

F. THE MESSIAH'S RESURRECTION AND ASCENSION

Old Testament Source	Prophecy	New Testament Fulfillment
"For You will not abandon my soul to Sheol [Hades]; nor will You allow Your Holy One to undergo decay." — Psalm 16:10 (Psalm 22:19-24 and Isaiah 53:10-11)	**1) Resurrection**	"And he [an angel] said to them, 'Do not be amazed; you are looking for Jesus the Nazarene, who has been crucified. He has risen; He is not here . . .'" — Mark 16:6 (Acts 2:31-32)
"You have ascended on high, You have led captive Your captives . . ." — Psalm 68:18	**2) Ascension**	"And after He had said these things, He was lifted up while they were looking on, and a cloud received Him out of their sight." — Acts 1:9 (Ephesians 4:7-10)
"The Lord says to my Lord: 'Sit at My right hand, until I make Your enemies a footstool for Your feet.'" — Psalm 110:1	**3) Exaltation at the right hand of God**	"So then, when the Lord Jesus had spoken to them, He was received up into heaven and sat down at the right hand of God." — Mark 16:19 (Acts 7:55-56 and Hebrews 1:3, 13)

Old Testament Source	Prophecy	New Testament Fulfillment
"The Lord has sworn and will not change His mind, 'You are a priest forever according to the order of Melchizedek.'" — Psalm 110:4	4) Serve as High Priest	". . . Jesus has entered as a fore-runner for us, having become a high priest according to the order of Melchizedek." — Hebrews 6:20 (Hebrews 5:1-7; and Hebrews 7: 11-28)
"Why are the nations in an uproar, and the people devising a vain thing? The kings of the earth take their stand and the rulers take counsel together against the Lord and against His Anointed . . ." — Psalm 2:1-2	5) Continue to be despised by the nations	". . . the whole world lies in the power of the evil one." — 1 John 5:19

Messiah Came According To God's Plan

B. FIRST ADVENT PROPHECIES IN THE NEW TESTAMENT

1. INTRODUCTION

Prophecies about the First Advent of the Messiah are not confined to the Old Testament. This is a truth that is often overlooked.

New Testament Sources

The Gospels contain a number of prophecies about the First Advent. A good number of them are clustered around the birth of Jesus.

Angels spoke prophecies about the Lord's First Coming to Joseph and Mary, to the priest Zacharias, and to the shepherds of Bethlehem. There were also several prophecies which the Holy Spirit prompted from people connected with the birth of Jesus — people like the parents of John the Baptist (Zacharias and Elizabeth), the Lord's mother, and two aged prophets named Simeon and Anna.

John the Baptist, who was a prophet of God, made several prophetic statements about his cousin, Jesus. And Caiaphas, the High Priest at the time of Jesus' death was directed by the Holy Spirit to make a prophetic utterance about the death of Jesus and its significance.

Jesus, "the Prophet"

The bulk of the New Testament prophecies concerning events related to the First Advent came from the mouth of Jesus Himself. Fifteen hundred years earlier, Moses had prophesied that the Messiah would be a prophet (Deuteronomy 18:15, 18). This is the reason that John the Baptist was asked if he was "the Prophet" (John 1:21). He denied that he was (John 1:22-23).

Later, when Jesus began His ministry, His miraculous signs caused the people to cry out, "This is truly the Prophet who is to come into the world" (John 6:14 and John 7:41).

Jesus certainly operated as a prophet. He spoke voluminous prophecies concerning His Second Advent. He also spoke prophetically about events that would occur during His First Advent — or which would result from it.

The Subject Matter

Concerning His First Coming, the topic He gave the most attention to was His death and resurrection. Repeatedly, He told His disciples that He would be killed and that He would rise from the dead on the third day after His death. Another topic He prophesied about in detail was the Holy Spirit. He stated that He would send the Spirit after His departure, and He prophesied what the work of the Spirit would be.

The Significance

The 100% accuracy of Jesus' prophecies about Himself are proof positive that He was God in the flesh. He was also totally accurate in His prophecies about individuals, the Jews, the Church, and the city of Jerusalem. There is no doubt that Jesus was "the Prophet" whom Moses told his people to watch for — the One who would also be the Messiah of God. ✤

2. OUTLINE OF FIRST ADVENT PROPHECIES IN THE NEW TESTAMENT

I. Prophecies by Angels

   A. An "angel of the Lord" to Joseph (Matthew 1:20-23)

      1) His betrothed, Mary, to have a son — verse 20.

      2) The son's name to be called Jesus — verse 20.

      3) He "will save His people from their sins" — verse 20.

   B. Gabriel to Zacharias (Luke 1:11-17)

      1) His wife to have a son — verse 13.

      2) The son's name to be John — verse 13.

      3) He will be filled with the Holy Spirit while in his mother's womb — verse 15.

      4) He will "turn back many of the sons of Israel to the Lord their God" — verse 16.

      5) He will serve as a forerunner of the Messiah — verse 17.

   C. Gabriel to Mary (Luke 1:26-37)

      1) She will conceive a son — verse 31.

      2) His name will be Jesus — verse 31.

      3) He will be great — verse 32.

      4) He will be called "the Son of the Most High" — verse 32.

      5) She will conceive by the power of the Holy Spirit — verse 35.

   D. Angels to the Shepherds of Bethlehem (Luke 2:8-14)

      Prophesied Jesus to be Savior to all people — verses 10-11.

II. Prophetic Statements by Individuals

A. Elizabeth (wife of Zacharias)

Prophesied that the baby in Mary's womb was the Lord.
Luke 1:43.

B. Mary (wife of Joseph)

Prophesied in a song of rejoicing that she was to give birth to the Messiah.
Luke 1:46-55.

C. Zacharias (husband of Elizabeth)

1) Prophesied that God had sent a Savior — "the Sunrise from on high."
Luke 1:68-73, 78-79.

2) His newborn son, John, would serve as a prophet, preparing the way for the Messiah.
Luke 1:76-77.

D. Simeon and Anna

When the baby Jesus was taken by his parents to the Temple in Jerusalem, both of these aged prophets proclaimed the baby to be the Savior of the Jews and the Gentiles. Luke 2:25-38.

E. John the Baptist

1) Prophesied the Messiah will be one who has existed eternally.
John 1:15, 30.

2) Stated his purpose was to prepare the way for the coming of the Messiah.
Matthew 3:3; Mark 1:7; and John 1:23.

3) Declared Jesus to be "the Lamb of God who takes away the sin of the world."
John 1:29, 36.

4) Prophesied Jesus would baptize with the Holy Spirit.
Matthew 3:11; Mark 1:8; Mark 3:16; and John 1:33.

5) Declared Jesus to be Savior.
John 3:36.

F. Caiaphas, the High Priest (who condemned Jesus to death)

Prophesied that one man would die for the people so that "the whole nation should not perish" (John 11:50). The next verse, John 11:51, says Caiaphas did not give this prophecy "on his own initiative" (in other words, it was inspired by God). Verse 51 also says this was a prophecy that Jesus would "die for the nation."

III. Prophecies by Jesus

A. Concerning His Purpose

1) That He came "to give His life a ransom for many."
Matthew 20:28 and Mark 10:45.

2) That He came to save the world and not to judge it.
John 3:17 and John 12:47.

B. Concerning the Law

That He came to fulfill the Law.
Matthew 5:17.

C. Concerning His Fate

1) Betrayal

a) To be "delivered" (betrayed) to His enemies.
Matthew 17:22; Matthew 20:18; Matthew 26:45-46; Mark 9:31; Mark 14:42;
Luke 9:44; and Luke 24:7.

b) To be betrayed by one of the Apostles.
Matthew 26:20-24; Mark 14:17-21; Luke 22:21-22; John 13:18-19, 21; and John
17:12.

2) Trial

a) To be rejected and condemned to death by the chief priests and scribes.
Matthew 20:18; Mark 8:31; Mark 10:33; and Luke 9:22.

b) To be delivered to the Gentiles for death.
Matthew 20:19; Mark 10:33; and Luke 18:32.

3) Suffering

a) To be mistreated.
Luke 12:50 and Luke 18:32.

b) To be mocked.
Matthew 20:19; Mark 10:34; and Luke 18:32.

c) To be spit upon.
Mark 10:34 and Luke 18:32.

d) To be scourged.
Matthew 20:19; Mark 10:34; and Luke 18:33.

      4) Death

          a) To be killed.
             Mark 8:31; Mark 9:31; Mark 10:34; Luke 9:22; and Luke 18:33.

          b) To be killed in Jerusalem.
             Matthew 16:21 and Mark 10:33.

          c) To be killed by crucifixion.
             Matthew 20:19; Matthew 26:2; and Luke 24:7.

          d) To die willingly.
             John 10:17-18 and John 15:13.

D. Concerning the Resurrection

    1) To fulfill the "sign of Jonah" by staying three days and nights "in the heart of the earth."
        Matthew 12:39-40; Matthew 16:4; and Luke 11:29-30.

    2) To be "raised up."
        Matthew 17:23; Matthew 26:32; Mark 9:9; and Luke 18:31.

    3) To be "raised up" on the third day after His death.
        Matthew 16:21; Matthew 17:23; Matthew 20:19; Mark 8:31; Mark 9:31; Mark 10:34; Luke 9:22; Luke 18:33; Luke 24:7; and John 2:19-22.

    4) To appear to His disciples in Galilee.
        Matthew 26:32.

E. Concerning His Disciples

    1) They would desert Him.
        Matthew 26:31 and Mark 14:27.

    2) Peter would deny Him three times.
        Matthew 26:33-34; Mark 14:30; and Luke 22:34, 61.

    3) Peter would be renewed after being tried by Satan and would strengthen the other disciples. Luke 22:31-32.

    4) The Apostles would be anointed by the Holy Spirit — "clothed with power from on high."
        Luke 24:49 and Acts 1:5, 8.

    5) Peter to be martyred.
        John 21:18-19.

F. Concerning the Jews

   1) His rejection by the Jews would result in God's wrath being poured out on the nation of Israel and the city of Jerusalem. Matthew 23:37-38; Matthew 24:2; Mark 13:2; Luke 13:34-35; Luke 19:41-44; Luke 21:5-6, 20-24; and Luke 23:28-30.

      a) Illustrated in the curse on the fig tree.
        Matthew 21:18-19. (See also Mark 11:12-14.)

      b) Illustrated in the parable of the vine growers.
        Matthew 21:33-46; Mark 12:1-12; and Luke 20:9-18.

   2) His rejection by the Jews would result in the kingdom being given to the Gentiles (in the spiritual form of the Church). Matthew 21:42-43 and John 10:16.

G. Concerning the Church

   1) The Church to be established upon Peter's confession that Jesus is the Messiah, "the Son of the Living God." Matthew 16:15-19.

   2) The Gospel to be preached to all the world.
      Matthew 28:19; Mark 16:15; Luke 24:47; and Acts 1:8.

   3) Believers to be able to perform miraculous signs in His name.
      Mark 16:17-18.

H. Concerning the Holy Spirit

   1) The Holy Spirit would be given when He (Jesus) departed.
      John 14:16-17; John 15:26; and John 16:7-14.

   2) The Holy Spirit will:

      a) Witness Jesus — John 15:26.

      b) Glorify Jesus — John 16:14.

      c) Serve as a teacher — John 14:26.

      d) Lead believers into truth — John 14:17; John 15:26; and John 16:13.

      e) Be a helper to believers — John 14:16; John 15:26 and John 16:7.

      f) "Convict the world concerning sin and righteousness and judgment" — John 16:8

      g) "Disclose what is to come" — John 16:13.

I. Concerning Salvation

   1) Those who put their faith in Him will be saved.
      John 3:14-16; John 6:40, 47; and John 11:25-26.

   2) He is the only way to God.
      John 14:6

J. Concerning His Ascension

That He would ascend to the Father after His resurrection.
John 20:17.

Part Two

THE SECOND ADVENT OF JESUS IN OLD TESTAMENT PROPHECY

"Let not your heart be troubled; believe in God, believe also in Me. In My Father's house are many dwelling places . . I go to prepare a place for you . . I will come again, and receive you to Myself; that where I am, there you may be also." — John 14:1-3

The Lion and the Lamb

A song by Mike Witte ©

Father God, the great "I Am,"
Sent His Son to be the lamb,
To reveal His loving grace
In Jesus' face.

His deity He laid aside.
He suffered and He died.
The silent Lamb bore sin's disgrace
In our place.

As this Man of Sorrows wept,
The Lion of Judah slept;
He who was to be a king,
Gave everything.

So the Lamb was slain, and yet,
The Lion of Judah conquered death.
He will return, and all Heaven sing,
"The Lion is King!"

Chorus:
And when the Lion comes,
The earth will tremble with fear.
When the Lion roars,
All creation will hear.
But when we stand
Before His royal majesty,
It is the Lamb
Every eye will see!
It is the Lamb
Every eye will see!

The Lion and the Lamb
Together in one man;
A wondrous mystery,
Jesus is He.

The Lamb's suffering fulfilled,
Now His kingdom He will build,
To rule and reign in majesty
Eternally.

A. INTRODUCTION

The scripture references in this section regarding the Second Advent of Jesus are arranged according to the words of the Lord which He spoke to His disciples following His resurrection:

> All things which are written about Me in the Law of Moses and the Prophets and the Psalms must be fulfilled. — Luke 24:44

Note that the Lord groups Old Testament prophecies into three broad categories: the Law, the Prophets, and the Psalms.

Three Divisions of Hebrew Scripture

"The Law" refers to the first five books of the Hebrew Scriptures, the books of Moses which are referred to by Jews today as the Torah. These books are also commonly referred to as the Pentateuch — a Greek term.

"The Psalms" was a term used to refer not only to the book of Psalms but also to all the poetic wisdom literature, including Job, Proverbs, Ecclesiastes, and the Song of Solomon.

"The Prophets" was a reference to a far greater volume of literature than what we normally think of today. We think of the Major and Minor Prophets. The Jews of the First Century used the term to refer to these books and others which we think of as being more historical than prophetic — books like Joshua, Judges, First and Second Samuel, the Kings, and the Chronicles.

In the pages that follow, we will survey the Second Coming prophecies in the Old Testament. We will group them as Jesus did — in three broad categories — and we will consider them in the order in which He referred to them.

Prophetic Fulfillment

But first, one final introductory note. Some people interpret Luke 24:44 to mean that all Old Testament prophecies regarding the Messiah were fulfilled in the First Advent of Jesus. That is not what Jesus said. He did not say that all the prophecies *had been* fulfilled. Rather, He said they *must be* fulfilled. They will not all be fulfilled until the Millennial reign has ended and the Eternal State has been inaugurated.

Peter and Paul both make this very clear in their writings. In 1 Peter 1:11 we are told that the prophets foretold two things about the Messiah: "The sufferings of Christ and the glories to follow." The suffering prophecies were fulfilled in the First Advent. The glory prophecies will be fulfilled at the Second Advent.

Paul makes it very clear in 1 Corinthians 15 that there are prophecies yet to be fulfilled. He says the end will come only after Jesus delivers the kingdom to the Father, and he says that will occur after the reign of Jesus has resulted in the abolition of all rule and all authority and power — and the abolition of death (1 Corinthians 15:24-26). ✤

B. THE LAW

The books of Moses do not contain much specific prophecy about the Messiah, but what they do contain is most significant.

The very first Messianic prophecy in the Pentateuch is one about the virgin birth — see Genesis 3:15. The greatest concentration of Messianic prophecy is contained in the Abrahamic Covenant. The covenant is stated several times, and these various statements contain both elaborations and refinements. The book of Genesis records seven times when God discussed this covenant with Abraham (see Genesis 12:1-3; 12:7; 13:14-16; 15: 4-6; 15:18-21; 17:1-14; and 22:15-18). Genesis records six other times when God renewed the covenant with either Isaac or Jacob (see Genesis 26:2-5; 26:23-24; 27: 27-29; 28:3-4; 28:13-14; and 35:9-12).

The Promises to Abraham

The prophecies contained in the Abrahamic Covenant relate to both the First and Second Advents of the Messiah. The prophecies are presented in the form of promises:

1) Abraham to become the father of a great nation.

2) Abraham's descendants to be as numerous as the dust of the earth and the stars in the sky.

3) Through Abraham all nations of the earth to be blessed.

4) A special land, the land of Canaan, to be given to the descendants of Abraham as an everlasting possession.

5) God to bless those who bless Abraham's descendants and curse those who curse them.

Specific Second Advent Prophecies

Apart from the Abrahamic Covenant, most of the specific Second Coming prophecies contained in the books of Moses are found in five passages:

1) The First Song of Moses (following the crossing of the Red Sea) — Exodus 15.

2) The Third and Fourth Prophecies of Balaam — Numbers 24.

3) The Speech of Moses in the Land of Moab — Deuteronomy 4.

4) The Land Covenant — Deuteronomy 28-30.

5) The Second Song of Moses (at the end of the Wilderness wanderings) — Deuteronomy 32.

The specific prophetic material contained in these passages is rather limited in quantity and scope. The First Song of Moses reveals only that the eternal abode of God will be Jerusalem where "the Lord shall reign forever and ever" (Exodus 15:17-18).

The third prophecy of Balaam gives us a brief glimpse of the redeemed Jews dwelling in peace and bounty as the exalted nation of the Millennium (Numbers 24:5-7). His fourth prophecy pictures the nations in judgment during the Tribulation (Numbers 24:17-24).

The Moab discourse of Moses, recorded in Deuteronomy 4, contains some pointed words about the Jews during the "latter days" (vs. 30). Moses says the Jews will experience a period of "distress" (the Tribulation) which will motivate them to "return to the Lord your God and listen to His voice" (vs. 30).

He says that at that point of repentance, the Lord will bless Israel by fulfilling His covenant promises to Abraham (vs. 31).

The Land Covenant

The Land Covenant of Deuteronomy 28-30 lays down the conditions for the Jew's possession and enjoyment of their Promised Land. It contains a prophetic panorama of Jewish history:

1) Dispersion among the nations as punishment for idolatry — Deuteronomy 28:58-64.

2) Persecution by the nations where the Jews are dispersed — Deuteronomy 28:65-67.

3) Affliction of the land of Israel until it becomes a "waste land" — Deuteronomy 29:22-28.

4) Repentance of the Jews — Deuteronomy 30:1-2.

5) Spiritual regeneration of the repenting remnant — Deuteronomy 30:6, 8.

6) Regathering of the Remnant to the land of promise — Deuteronomy 30:3-4. (Note: This is the regathering in belief that will take place at the Second Advent. It is not the regathering in unbelief that is going on now.)

7) Repossession of the Promised Land by the Jews — Deuteronomy 30:5.

8) Punishment of the enemies of Israel — Deuteronomy 30:7.

9) Blessing of the re-established nation of Israel with material prosperity — Deuteronomy 30:5, 9.

A Song of Moses

The Second Song of Moses reveals the Messiah as "the Rock" (Deuteronomy 32:4, 15, 18, 30-31). The Song prophesies Israel's unfaithfulness (vs. 5, 15-18) and God's decision to set them aside and work instead through the Church (vs. 19-21). The song gives us a glimpse of the horrors of the Tribulation (vs. 23-27) as God pours out His wrath to bring the Jews to repentance.

Just as the song leads us to believe there is no hope for the Jews, it suddenly reveals the glorious grace of God in His salvation of the remnant: ". . . the Lord will vindicate His people, and will have compassion on His servants . . ." (Deuteronomy 32:36). The Lord Himself sums up His action by saying, "I have wounded, and it is I who heal . . ." (vs. 39).

The song concludes with the nations being exhorted to praise God for His salvation and restoration of Israel — both the people and the land (vs. 43):

> Rejoice, O nations, with His
>   people;
> For He will avenge the blood of
>   His servants,
> And will render vengeance on
>   His adversaries,
> And will atone for His land and
>   His people.

Graphic Prophecies of God's Wrath

The Pentateuch closes with Moses pronouncing a blessing upon each of the tribes of Israel. He begins this blessing by reminding them of the Lord's appearance in the Wilderness (Deuteronomy 33:2):

> The Lord came from Sinai,
> And dawned on them from Seir;
> He shone forth from Mount
>   Paran,
> And He came from the midst of
>   ten thousand holy ones;
> At His right hand there was
>   flashing lightning for them.

We know from other prophecies in the Old Testament that this description of the Lord's coming in the Wilderness is also a prophetic description of the Lord's Second Advent. Compare, for example, the similar descriptions of the Lord's Second Coming that are recorded in Isaiah 63:1-6 and Habakkuk 3:3-15. All three of these passages use similar language to describe the Lord's return from the East in wrath. *This statement by Moses thus stands out as the first prophetic description in the Bible of the Lord's Second Advent.*

However, there is another prophetic description of the Second Coming that is older than the Mosaic one in Deuteronomy. It is found, strangely enough, in the New Testament, in the book of Jude, beginning with verse 14, where it says that Enoch, in the seventh generation from Adam, prophesied, saying:

> Behold, the Lord came with many thousands of His holy ones, to execute judgment upon all, and to convict all the ungodly of all their ungodly deeds which they have done in an ungodly way, and of all the harsh things which ungodly sinners have spoken against Him.

This prophecy was pre-filled in type in the devastation of the Flood. It will be fulfilled in the wrath which God will pour out at the Second Advent of His Son.

Prophetic Types

Paul wrote that things in the Hebrew Scriptures are a "mere shadow of what is to come" (Galatians 2:17). He then adds that "the substance belongs to Christ."

Paul is speaking here of what we call prophetic types or symbolic prophecy. Most of the Second Coming prophecy in the Law is symbolic prophecy in type. It falls into four broad categories: human types, historical types, ceremonial types, and types based on inanimate objects.

✔ Human Types

1. **Abel** — Like Jesus, Abel was an innocent victim of murder whose blood cries out for the vengeance which God will execute when Jesus returns (Hebrews 10:28-31 and Hebrews 11:4).

2. **Melchizedek** — He was both a priest and a king (Genesis 14:18), as Jesus will be when He returns (Zechariah 6:13). His name means "King of Righteousness" (Hebrews 7:2), and Jesus will be a righteous king when He returns (Isaiah 11:5 and 32:1). In fact, Jesus's name will be changed when He returns to "Yahweh Tsidkenu," meaning "The Lord our Righteousness" (Jeremiah 23:6). Melchizedek was "King of Salem" (Genesis 14:18), meaning "Prince of Peace," just as Jesus will be when He returns. (Isaiah 9:6).

3. **Enoch** — His supernatural departure from the world before the Flood (Genesis 5:24) is a type of the Rapture of the Church before the Tribulation.

4. **Isaac** — His father Abraham's search for an appropriate bride is prophetic of the Rapture. The father sends a servant (the Holy Spirit) to bring a bride (the Church) to his son (the Bridegroom-King) — see Genesis 24.

5. **Joseph** — Every aspect of Joseph's life points to a parallel event in the life of the Messiah. Like Jesus, Joseph was rejected by his brethren. He then experienced a symbolic death and resurrection as his brothers abandoned him in a pit, declared him to be dead, and he was rescued by a passing caravan. He took a Gentile bride (even as Jesus is now preparing His Gentile Bride, the Church). Then Joseph manifested himself to his brethren and saved them from famine — just as Jesus will reveal Himself to the Jews at His Second Coming and will bring salvation to a remnant. — See Genesis 37-46.

6. **Moses** — Like Joseph (and Jesus), Moses was rejected by his people (the Jews). He then took a Gentile bride (just as Jesus is doing now) and returned to deliver his people (as Jesus will do). They accepted him and were delivered from bondage (just as the Jewish remnant will accept Jesus as Messiah when He returns) — See Zechariah 12:10.

7. **Aaron** — As High Priest of Israel, he pointed to Jesus who serves currently as our High Priest before the throne of God. Jesus will continue to serve as High Priest when He returns to rule the world as King of kings.

✔ Historical Types

1. **The Creation Week** — God created the heavens and the earth in six days. On the seventh day, the Sabbath, He rested. This pattern of six days of toil followed by one day of rest is repeated many times in the ceremonies and festivals of the Jews. For example, God told Israel to work the land only six years in a row. The land was to lie fallow every seventh year, taking its Sabbath rest (Leviticus 23:3-4).

   In like manner, the Jews celebrated seven feasts each year. The first six were related in part to the agricultural cycle — the planting, growing, and harvesting of various crops. The seventh, the Feast of Tabernacles, was a feast of rest for seven days (Leviticus 23:34-36). It celebrated the completion of the agricultural cycle.

   This pattern of six days of toil and one day of rest was interpreted by the Rabbis long before the birth of Jesus to be a prophecy in type that human history would consist of six thousand years of toil followed by one thousand years of rest (the Millennium).

   The Bible records two thousand years from Adam to Abraham and two thousand years from Abraham to Jesus. As we approach two thousand years since the time of Jesus, we also approach the end of the six thousand years of human toil and strife that should usher in the one thousand years of Sabbath rest.

2. **The Destruction of Sodom and Gomorrah** (Genesis 19) — God's provision for the supernatural departure of Lot and his family before the destruction of the cities is a type of the Rapture of the Church before the Tribulation begins.

3. **Noah's Society** (Genesis 6) — It was "corrupt in the sight of God" (Genesis 6: 11). It was characterized by violence and immorality. Wickedness was great and "every intent of the thoughts of [man's] heart was only evil continually" (vs. 5). Jesus said that He would return at a time when the world would once again be like it was in the time of Noah (Matthew 24:37-39). Noah's society was a type of the end time society that will prevail worldwide when Jesus returns.

4. **Destruction of the World by Water** (Genesis 7) — It is a type of the pouring out of God's wrath that the world will once again experience during the Tribulation and at the end of the Millennium when God will destroy the earth with fire.

   A second type is included in the story of the Flood. God's protection of Noah and his family in the Ark during the flood is a type of the protection that God will provide the Jewish remnant through the period of the Tribulation.

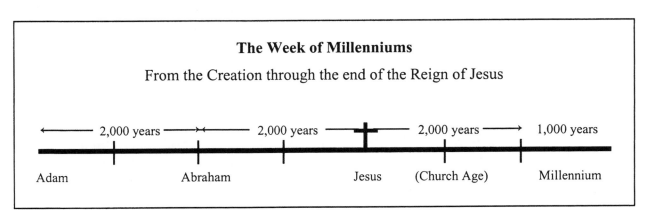

The Week of Millenniums

From the Creation through the end of the Reign of Jesus

← 2,000 years →	← 2,000 years —	— 2,000 years →	1,000 years
Adam	Abraham	Jesus (Church Age)	Millennium

Another prophetic type that can be drawn from the flood story is based on the fact that Enoch was raptured out of the world before the flood began (Genesis 5:24). Enoch is thus a type of the Church that will be raptured before the Tribulation begins.

5. **The Tower of Babel** (Genesis 11) — "Come, let us build for ourselves a city, and a tower whose top will reach into heaven, and let us make for ourselves a name . . ." (vs. 4). It is a type of the Humanistic, one-world unity movement that will characterize the end times, culminating in the establishment of the worldwide empire of the Antichrist (Revelation 13:7-8).

✔ **Ceremonial Types**

1. **The Feasts** (Leviticus 23) — As illustrated on the next page, the seven feasts which were celebrated each year by the Jews were all prophetic symbols pointing to events that would occur in the Christian era:

   1) Passover — The Crucifixion of Jesus

   2) Unleavened Bread — The Burial of Jesus

   3) First Fruits — The Resurrection of Jesus

   4) Pentecost — The Establishment of the Church

   5) Trumpets — The Rapture of the Church (?)

   6) Day of Atonement —The Second Advent of Jesus (?)

   7) Tabernacles — The Millennial Reign of Jesus (?)

   The first four of these feasts were fulfilled in the First Century on the very day of each feast. The last three relate to the Second Advent and are yet to be fulfilled. I think we can safely assume that like the first four feasts, these last three will be fulfilled on the actual day of their celebration.

As to exactly how they will be fulfilled, we can only guess. The Day of Trumpets most likely points to the Rapture of the Church since the Rapture is associated in Scripture with the blowing of a trumpet (1 Corinthians 15:52 and 1 Thessalonians 4:16). The Day of Atonement would seem to point to the Second Advent since it is on that day that the Jewish Remnant will experience the salvation of the Messiah (Zechariah 12:10). There doesn't seem to be much doubt about the prophetic significance of Tabernacles because the Jews have always celebrated it as a promise of God that He would someday return to tabernacle with Mankind upon the earth.

2. **The Jubilee** (Leviticus 25) — The Jubilee Year is a type of the Millennial reign of the Messiah, for it was a year of justice, equity, plenty, rest, and celebration.

3. **Marriage Rites** (Deuteronomy 22 and 24) — With the giving of the Law, the Jews began to develop new marriage traditions that ultimately culminated in a four part process: The Betrothal; The Fetching; The Ceremony; and The Feast.

The betrothal, or marriage agreement, was negotiated by the parents and sealed with a price — a dowry payment. It was followed by a waiting period of nine months to a year. During this time the groom built a room onto his father's house where he and his new bride would live. As the bride waited for her bridegroom to come for her, she proved her faithfulness.

When the bridegroom was ready, he would gather his friends and proceed to the bride's house to fetch her. A loud trumpet would be blown to announce his coming. The bride and groom would return to the house of the groom's father where they would enter the bridal cham-

The Christian Meaning Of The Jewish Feasts

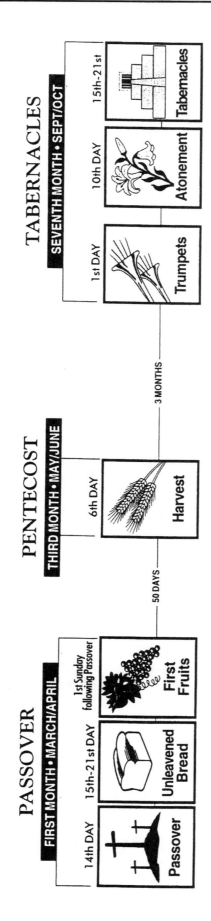

PASSOVER
FIRST MONTH • MARCH/APRIL

14th DAY — Passover

15th-21st DAY — Unleavened Bread

1st Sunday following Passover — First Fruits

50 DAYS

PENTECOST
THIRD MONTH • MAY/JUNE

6th DAY — Harvest

3 MONTHS

TABERNACLES
SEVENTH MONTH • SEPT/OCT

1st DAY — Trumpets

10th DAY — Atonement

15th-21st — Tabernacles

FEAST

Passover ....
Unleavened Bread ....
First Fruits ....
Harvest ....
Interval of 3 Months .....
Trumpets ....
Day of Atonement ....
Tabernacles ....

CHRISTIAN EVENT

Crucifixion of Jesus ....
Burial of Jesus ....
Resurrection of Jesus ....
Descent of Holy Spirit ....
Current Age of the Church ....
Gathering of the Church (?) ....
Second Coming of Jesus (?) ....
Inauguration of the Millennium ....

KEY CONCEPT

Justification
Sanctification
Glorification
Power
Church Kingdom
Rapture
Jewish Remnant
Earthly Kingdom

ber and consummate the marriage. After seven days they would come out of the chamber, and they and all their friends would celebrate the marriage with a joyous marriage feast.

All of this tradition is a prophetic type pointing to Jesus and His Bride, the Church. The Father paid the betrothal price with the blood of His Son (Ephesians 5:25-27). The Bride is now waiting for her fetching (the Rapture) by the Bridegroom (1 Thessalonians 4:13-18). As the Bride waits, the Bridegroom (Jesus) is preparing a glorious mansion (the new Jerusalem) to house His Bride (John 14:1-3). The seven days in the bridal chamber point to the seven years that the Bride will be in Heaven with her Bridegroom, during the time of the Tribulation. The marriage feast will occur in Heaven at the end of the Tribulation, right before Jesus returns to the earth with His Bride (Revelation 19:5-16).

✔ **Inanimate Objects** —

Even inanimate objects in the Hebrew Scriptures often serve as prophetic types. Let's consider two examples.

1. **The Tabernacle of Moses** — This is the example most people think of because there has been such widespread teaching about it. Every aspect of the Tabernacle was a "shadow" of the Messiah and His work.

   The door into the Tabernacle's outer court pointed to Jesus as the door leading to the Father and eternal life (John 10:9). The altar stood for the sacrifice the Messiah would have to make. The laver symbolized the washing and regeneration in the Word and the Holy Spirit that would be experienced by believers in Jesus (Ephesians 5:26 and Titus 3:5). Inside the Holy Place, the table of shewbread pointed to the Messiah as the "bread of life" (John 6:35), and the menorah proclaimed that the Messiah would be the "light of

the world" (John 8:12). The incense before the curtain separating the Holy Place from the Holy of Holies symbolized the role of the Messiah after His resurrection — the role He plays today as our High Priest before the throne of God, interceding for the saints in response to their prayers. (See Figure 2 on page 9.)

2. **The Ark of the Covenant** — Inside the Holy of Holies was the sacred Ark. It too was symbolic of the Messiah. It was made of acacia wood which pointed to the Messiah's humanity. The wood was overlaid with gold to signify that the Messiah would also be divine.

   Inside the Ark were three things: the tablets of the Law given to Moses, a pot of manna, and Aaron's rod that budded (Exodus 25:10-22 and Hebrews 9:4). The tablets of the Law pictured the Messiah with the Law of God in His heart, living in perfect obedience to it. The pot of manna spoke of the Messiah as the bread of life or our life sustainer. Aaron's rod that budded obviously prophesied the resurrection of the Messiah.

   The "mercy seat," which served as a lid or cover for the top of the Ark, was also a symbol that pointed to the Messiah. Once a year the high priest would enter the Holy of Holies and sprinkle blood on the mercy seat to atone for the sins of the people (Leviticus 16 and Hebrews 9). This act was representative of the fact that the Messiah would need to shed His blood to make it possible for the mercy of God to cover the Law of God. The high priest also sprinkled blood on the ground in front of the Ark (Leviticus 16:15). This act symbolized the fact that the Messiah would die not only for Man but for the redemption of all creation.

   At each end of the mercy seat were two golden angels, facing each other with outstretched wings. The Shekinah glory of God resided above these angels (1 Samuel 4:4 and Isaiah 37:16).

Jesus fulfilled the prophetic symbolism of the Ark in His life and death and resurrection. He was God in the flesh, living in perfect obedience to the Law and providing life to all who put their faith in Him.

When Mary Magdalene went to the tomb of Jesus and found it empty, she saw "two angels sitting, one at the head and one at the feet, where the body of Jesus had been lying" (John 20:12). She saw the place where the blood of the Messiah had been spilled, and there was an angel at each end — exactly like the mercy seat on top of the Ark. Mary saw the fulfillment of what the Ark of the Covenant stood for.

As these prophecies in type clearly illustrate, Jesus can be found in almost every chapter of the Law, if you know how to look for Him. I think this is what Paul had in mind when he wrote these words to Timothy: "From childhood you have known the sacred writings which are able to give you the wisdom that leads to salvation through faith which is in Christ Jesus" (2 Timothy 3:15).

The only "sacred writings" that existed at the time Paul wrote these words were the Hebrew Scriptures which we call the Old Testament. In other words, Paul says that a person can be led to faith in Christ through a study of the Old Testament.

An Example of
Symbolic Prophecy in Action

The New Testament presents us with an excellent example of the use of symbolic prophecy to bring a person to salvation. It is found in the story of Phillip and the Ethiopian Eunuch, recorded in Acts 8:25-40.

An angel appeared to the evangelist Phillip and told him to go to the road that runs from Jerusalem to Gaza. When Phillip arrived at the road, he encountered a Jew from Ethiopia who was returning home after going to Jerusalem to worship. Phillip heard the man reading from Isaiah 53. He asked him if he understood what he was reading. The Ethiopian answered, "Well, how could I, unless someone guides me?"

At this point Phillip got in the Ethiopian's chariot and began to expound the meaning of Isaiah 53. The result was that the Ethiopian accepted Jesus as his savior, he was immediately baptized, and he went on his way rejoicing.

Now, what was the nature of the passage that Phillip used to convert this man? It was symbolic prophecy in which the Messiah is presented as a suffering lamb. What Phillip did was show the Ethiopian that the symbolic imagery pointed to Jesus who had come as the "Lamb of God" (John 1:29) to die for the sins of Mankind. ✤

"The Law has become our tutor to lead us to Christ." — Galatians 3:24

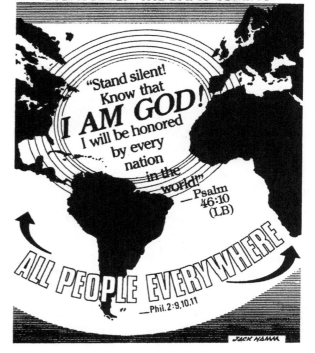

EVENTUALLY—THE DAY IS COMING

C. THE PROPHETS

1. INTRODUCTION

This chapter presents an analytical summary of Old Testament prophecies concerning the Second Advent which are contained in the books which the Jews generally classify as "The Prophets." This includes the Major and Minor Prophets (Isaiah through Malachi) and the Historical Books (Joshua through Esther).

The Historical Books

There is actually very little specific Second Coming prophecy in the Historical Books. Nearly all of it is contained in six passages — two covenant statements and four poems:

1) The two statements of the Davidic Covenant — 2 Samuel 7 and 1 Chronicles 17.

2) Hannah's prayer of thanksgiving for her son — 1 Samuel 2.

3) David's song of praise for deliverance from Saul — 2 Samuel 22.

4) David's psalm of thanksgiving for the deliverance of the Ark to Jerusalem — 1 Chronicles 16.

5) David's death bed testamentary psalm — 2 Samuel 23.

There is, of course, much prophecy in type contained in the Historical Books, particularly as symbolized in the lives of various individuals. Most of this typology relates to the First Advent (see pages 7-10). However, there are some significant types that relate to the Second Advent.

Prophetic Types

There are six individuals who appear in "The Prophets" whose lives are prophetic of various aspects of the Second Advent. Two are well known. They are David and Solomon. The other four are rather obscure figures. They are Eliakim, Cyrus, Zerubbabel, and a priest named Joshua.

David and Solomon

David typifies the Messiah in many ways. As a shepherd-king he points to the Millennial reign when Jesus will serve as both Spiritual Shepherd and King of kings. Before becoming king, David served a long time as a king-in-waiting. He had been anointed king by Samuel, but he had to wait many years before he became the King of Judah. Likewise, Jesus has been anointed the King of kings, but He is now waiting for His coronation. He will not take up His rule until His Father sends Him back to reign from Mt. Zion in Jerusalem (Psalm 2).

The glory and majesty of Solomon's reign is a type of the glory the whole world will experience when Jesus begins His reign. The marvelous nature of that glory is reflected in Solomon's majestic prayer in Psalm 72.

Images for Isaiah

Isaiah presents a scribe by the name of Eliakim as a type of the Messiah (Isaiah 22:15-25). He is presented as "a father to the inhabitants of Jerusalem and to the house of Judah" (vs. 21). And to him is given "the key of the house of David" (vs. 22). It is prophesied that he will "become a throne of glory to his father's house" and that on him "they will hang all the glory of his father's house" (vs. 23-24). In Revelation 3:7 Jesus identifies Himself as the one who has the key of David. So, Eliakim is a picture of the authority and glory which will be given to the resurrected Messiah when He returns to reign from the throne of David.

Isaiah presents another Christ figure in chapters 44 and 45. The person is Cyrus, referred to as the Lord's "anointed" (45:1). This is a most unusual prophetic type because the Cyrus who prefilled this prophecy was a Gentile — the only Gentile in Scripture referred to as God's anointed. In this prophecy Isaiah says a man by the name of Cyrus will serve as God's "shepherd" by declaring that Jerusalem will be rebuilt (44:28).

About 150 years after Isaiah spoke this prophecy, a man named Cyrus was born and became the head of the Medo-Persian Empire which overthrew Babylon. At that time the Jews were in Babylonian captivity. Cyrus was the one who released them and sent them home to rebuild Jerusalem (Ezra 1:1-3 and 5:13). Like Cyrus, Jesus will return to deliver the Jewish Remnant from their spiritual bondage and will then lead them in rebuilding the city of Jerusalem and the Temple (Zechariah 1:16-17; 2:4-5; and 6:12-13).

Images for Haggai and Zechariah

The prophet Haggai presents Zerubbabel, the post-Babylon governor of Judah, as a type of the Messiah (Haggai 2:20-23). He states that God will overthrow all kingdoms before him and make him His "signet ring" (vs. 22-23). This prophecy will be fulfilled when Jesus is installed as King of kings on Mt. Zion. He will then be the signet ring of God in the sense that He will reign with God's authority (Psalm 2).

The prophet Zechariah presents the last of the Messianic types when he singles out Joshua, the son of the High Priest, Jehozadak (Zechariah 3:6-10 and 6:9-13). He calls Joshua "the Branch," which is a Messianic title used by Isaiah (Isaiah 4:2 and 11:1) and Jere-

miah (Jeremiah 23:5 and 33:15) to emphasize that the Messiah will be a branch from the stem of Jesse (Isaiah 11:1) — that is, He will be from the House of David (Jeremiah 33:15). Zechariah then prophesies that "the Branch" will rebuild the Temple and reign as both priest and king (Zechariah 6:12-13). Jesus will fulfill this prophecy when He returns, for He will rebuild the Temple, and He will serve as both High Priest and King of kings.

Scope of the Outline

The specific prophecies recorded in the following detailed outline are the ones which concern events from the time of the Rapture through the end of the Millennium, or the beginning of the Eternal State. This is the period of time that is often referred to in Scripture as "The day of the Lord" (Joel 1:15 and 2 Thessalonians 2:2).

However, it should be kept in mind that this term is sometimes used to refer to specific days or periods of time. In Joel 2:31 it is used to refer to the exact day that the Lord's Second Coming will take place. In Isaiah 2:12-19 and Jeremiah 30:4-7, it is used in reference to the Tribulation. In chapters 4, 12, and 19 of Isaiah, and in Jeremiah 30:8-11, it refers to the Millennium. In the New Testament, in 1 Thessalonians 5:2 and 2 Thessalonians 2:2, it is used in the broad sense to designate the period from the Rapture to the end of the Millennium. Like the Rapture, it is a signless event that will come upon the world "like a thief in the night" (1 Thessalonians 5:2).

The Eternal State is referred to in Scripture as "the day of God" (2 Peter 3:12). We are currently in the day of the Holy Spirit (2 Corinthians 3:8). The "day of the Lord" falls between the day of the Holy Spirit and the day of God, stretching from the Rapture to the conclusion of the Millennium.

The Rapture

One of the most important end time prophetic events associated with the Second

Coming of the Lord is the Rapture of the Church. This event is not specifically prophesied in the Old Testament, although it is clearly symbolized in type in the rapture of Enoch, and the fetching of Lot (see page 46). It is also typified in the Jewish marriage rites (pages 48 and 50) and in the marriage imagery of Psalm 45 (page 71).

I have indicated two passages in the outline where some scholars feel that the Rapture is alluded to. However, it is my judgment that the specific revelation of the Rapture was kept hidden from the Old Testament prophets. This is understandable because the Rapture is a promise to the Church, not to the Old Testament saints. The Church was a mystery to the Hebrew prophets (Ephesians 3:8-10 and Colossians 1:24-26). Old Testament saints will be resurrected at the end of the Tribulation (Daniel 12:1-2), not at the time of the Rapture.

The Rapture is not specifically referred to prophetically until Jesus' reference to it in John 14:1-3. It is revealed in detail for the first time in Paul's writings (1 Thessalonians 4:13-18 and 1 Corinthians 15:51-55).

Prefilled Prophecy

Some of the prophecies presented in the outline have been prefilled in history, but await an ultimate fulfillment. The prophecies regarding Babylon are the best example of this principle. They were prefilled in the destruction of the actual city of Babylon, but the book of Revelation makes it clear that they will ultimately be fulfilled in the end time destruction of the world empire of the Anti-christ (Revelation 17 and 18).

A Myth

One myth which the following prophetic outline clearly explodes is the idea that a future reign of the Lord on this earth is found only in the 20th chapter of Revelation. The Lord's earthly reign of peace, righteousness, and justice is one of the most prolific images of the Old Testament prophets. Revelation 20 simply fleshes out some of the details of prophecies already given in the Old Testament. Revelation is primarily a book about the Tribulation. Isaiah is the prophet of the Millennium. Daniel is the prophet of the Antichrist.

The Interregnum

Concerning what I have labeled "The Post Tribulation Period" (Section V of the outline on pages 60-61), it is my belief that the events outlined there will take place during the special 75 day period which Daniel says will follow the conclusion of the Tribulation period. (Daniel 12:12).

Daniel actually identifies two special periods of time. One extends 30 days beyond the end of the Great Tribulation (Daniel 12:11). The other extends an additional 45 days (Daniel 12:12), making a total period of 75 days. We cannot be certain what will happen during these periods, but most likely, the judgment of the living Gentiles and Jews will occupy the first 30 days, and the establishment of the Lord's millennial government will take up the next 45 days. Thus, this 75 day period will be a sort of interregnum between the Lord's return and the institution of His formal world government. "Interregnum" is a political term that refers to the period of transition between one government and another. This 75 day period of time will mark the transition between the government of the Antichrist and the government of Jesus Christ.

New Heavens and Earth

Concerning Isaiah's references to the "new heavens and earth," my studies have led me to the conclusion that the reference in Isaiah 65:17 definitely pertains to the Millennium rather than to the Eternal State. The same may be true of Isaiah 66:22, but it is not quite so clear, and so in the outline I have applied it to the Eternal State.

The Isaiah 65:17 reference to "new heavens and earth" has always intrigued me because it appears in the middle of a passage that is clearly talking about the Millennium. I had always identified it with the "new heavens and earth" referred to in Revelation 21, but that identification bothered me because Revelation 21 pictures the eternal earth, renovated by fire, whereas Isaiah 65:17 seems to be talking about the millennial earth. When I finally decided to accept the contextual meaning of the Isaiah 65 reference and therefore apply it to the Millennium, a whole new concept crystallized in my mind.

It suddenly occurred to me that the Lord intends to renovate the earth **twice** in the future, once for the Millennium and again for the Eternal State. God has already radically altered the earth twice: once with the Curse and once with water (the Noahic Flood). I now believe He is going to change it again in a radical way when Jesus returns to reign. This will be done through earthquakes on earth and supernatural phenomena in the heavens (Revelation 6:12-17 and 16:17-21). See Section VI-B of the following outline (page 63) for more details about the nature of the "new earth" on which Jesus will reign.

At the end of the Millennium, God will use fire to burn away the pollution of Satan's last revolt. (See Revelation 20:7-11 and Revelation 21:1. See also 2 Peter 3:10-13). I believe the earth we are on now will be superheated, becoming like a hot ball of wax. God will then reshape the earth into the "new earth" where we will spend eternity with God in our glorified bodies.

To summarize, the original, perfect earth (Earth I) was radically changed by the curse that God placed upon it in response to the sin of Adam and Eve, producing Earth II. The earth was radically transformed again by the Noahic Flood, producing Earth III, the one we live on now. The current earth will be destroyed and reshaped at the Second Coming of Jesus by earthquakes and supernatural phenomena in the heavens, producing Earth IV — the "new earth" of Isaiah 65 which Jesus will reign upon. That earth will be consumed with fire at the end of the Lord's reign, and out of that fiery renovation will come Earth V, the "new earth" of eternity. In other words, there are going to be two "new earths" in the future, not just the one referred to in Revelation 21. ✚

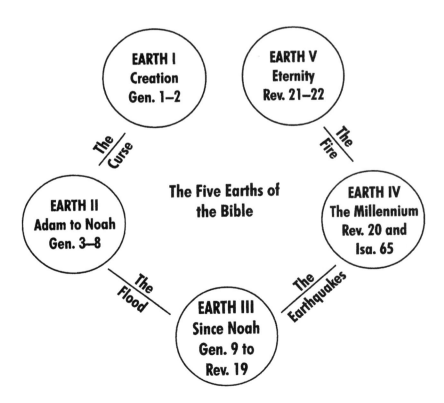

2. AN OUTLINE OF SECOND ADVENT PROPHECIES IN THE WRITINGS OF THE OLD TESTAMENT PROPHETS

(Joshua through Esther and Isaiah through Malachi)

Please note that the **sequence** of the end time events as presented in the following outline is determined to a large degree by New Testament revelations which will be outlined in Section Three.

I. Signs of the End Times

    A. The Understanding of Bible Prophecy
        Daniel 12:4, 8-9.

    B. The Revival of Davidic Praise Worship — "In that day I will raise up the fallen tabernacle of David . . ." Amos 9:11.

    C. A Great Outpouring of the Holy Spirit — "the latter rain"
        Joel 2:21-29.

    D. An Increase in Knowledge and Transportation
        Daniel 12:4.

    E. Europe Reunited in a Resurrection of the Roman Empire
        Daniel 2 and 7.

    F. Signs Related to the Jewish People

        1) The world-wide regathering of the Jews in unbelief to the land of Israel.
            Isaiah 11:10-12; Isaiah 43:4-7; Jeremiah 16:14-15; Jeremiah 23:7-8; Jeremiah 24:4-7; Jeremiah 30:1-3; Jeremiah 46:27; Ezekiel 11:16-17; Ezekiel 36:22-24; Ezekiel 37:1-12; and Amos 9:14-15.

        2) The re-establishment of the state of Israel.
            Isaiah 52:8-10; Isaiah 66:7-8; and Zechariah 12:1-3, 6.

        3) The revival of the Hebrew language.
            Zephaniah 3:9. (See also Jeremiah 31:23.)

        4) The reclamation of the land.
            Isaiah 35:1-2, 6-7; Isaiah 41:18-20; Isaiah 51:3; and Ezekiel 36:33-36. (These prophecies indicate that God always blesses the land when the Jews are in it — as He is doing today. The ultimate fulfillment of these prophecies will occur during the mllennial reign of Jesus.)

        5) The re-occupation of Jerusalem.
            Isaiah 52:1-3; Zechariah 12:2-3, 6, 9; Zechariah 14:1-2. (See Luke 21:24.)

6) The resurgence of Jewish military power.
Isaiah 41:15 and Zechariah 12:6, 8.

7) The re-focusing of world politics upon the nation of Israel and the city of Jerusalem.
Zechariah 12:3 and Zechariah 14:1-2.

8) Israel surrounded by enemies.

   a) A nation in "the remote parts of the north."
   Ezekiel 38, note especially verses 6 and 15.

   b) Nations allied with the northern power.
   Ezekiel 38:1-6.

   c) The Arab nations.
   Ezekiel 35:1 - 36:7.

   d) All the nations of the world.
   Zechariah 12:3.

II. The Rapture of the Church

Isaiah 57:1-2 (?). Joel 2:16 (?). Micah 7:2 (?). Note: The Rapture is a promise to the Church, not to Old Testament saints. It is therefore doubtful that any of these passages refer to the Rapture. See pages 53-54 for a discussion of this point.

III. The Tribulation

A. The Period of Time
Isaiah 2:12; Jeremiah 30:7; Ezekiel 22:17-22; Daniel 9:26-27; Daniel 12:1; Zechariah 13:8-9; and Malachi 3:1-4.

B. Elijah to be Sent to Call People to Repentance (One of the two witnesses of Revelation 11?) Malachi 4:5.

C. Russia Invades Israel and is Supernaturally Destroyed
Ezekiel 38:1- 39:16. Nebuchadnezzar's invasion of Judah is a possible prophetic type of the end time Russian invasion portrayed in Ezekiel 38 and 39. See Jeremiah 1:14-19; Jeremiah 4:5-9; and Jeremiah 6:22-26. See also Joel 1 and 2.

D. The Antichrist

   1) He will emerge from a 10 nation confederacy based in the same geographic area as the Roman Empire. Daniel 2:41-44 and Daniel 7:7-8, 24-26.

   2) He will be bold, clever, and a flatterer.
   Daniel 8:23-25 and Daniel 11:21.

3) He will be ruthless.
   Zechariah 11:15-16.

4) He will be crippled by a severe wound.
   Zechariah 11:17.

5) He will be prideful like Satan.
   Isaiah 14:12-16 and Ezekiel 28:11-19.

6) He will make a covenant with Israel which he will violate at the end of three and one-half years ("a time, times, and a half time"). Daniel 7:25; Daniel 9:27; and Daniel 11:23.

7) He will defile the Temple and stop the sacrifices.
   Daniel 8:11; Daniel 9:27; Daniel 11:31; and Daniel 12:11.

8) He will blaspheme God.
   Daniel 7:25; Daniel 8:11, 25; and Daniel 11:36-38.

9) He will try to change the calendar and the laws of God.
   Daniel 7:25.

10) He will trample the truth.
    Daniel 8:12.

11) He will wage war on the saints for three and one-half years.
    Daniel 7:20-22, 25 and Daniel 8:24.

12) He will accumulate great power and will use it to wage war among the nations.
    Daniel 8:24-25 and Daniel 11:22-25.

13) He will be attacked by armies from the north and south, but he will triumph over both and will conquer all the Holy Land except Edom and Moab. Daniel 11:40-41.

14) Just as he seems secure, he will be alarmed by tidings from the east and north and will meet his end while he is encamped "between the seas" (the Valley of Armageddon, located between the Mediterranean Sea and the Sea of Galilee). Daniel 11:44-45.

15) He will be destroyed.
    Isaiah 10:12-19 (The King of Assyria is a type of the Antichrist); Isaiah 14:12-17 (The King of Babylon is also a type of the Antichrist); Isaiah 24:21-23; Jeremiah 25:32-34; Daniel 7:11, 26; Daniel 11:45; Joel 2:20; Joel 3:12-16; Habakkuk 3:13-14; and Zechariah 14:1-3, 12-15.

E. Judgments

1) Upon the nations.
Isaiah 2:12-22; Isaiah 24:1-13; Isaiah 26:21; Isaiah 34:2-3; Jeremiah 10:25; Jeremiah 25:15-29; Obadiah 15-16; Habakkuk 3:6-15; Zephaniah 2:4-15; Zephaniah 3:8; Haggai 2:6-7, 21-22; Zechariah 1:18-21; Zechariah 6:1-8; and Malachi 4:1.

2) Upon the Jews (two-thirds to perish).
Isaiah 30:19-20; Isaiah 54:7-8; Jeremiah 4:23-31; Jeremiah 30:5-7; Jeremiah 46:28; Ezekiel 22:17-22; Daniel 12:1-2; Amos 9:9-10; Micah 7:2-7; Zephaniah 1:1-13; Zephaniah 3:11; Zechariah 5:1-4; Zechariah 13:7-9; and Malachi 3:2-5.

3) Upon Babylon (as a type of the Antichrist's religious, political, and economic system). Isaiah 13, 14, 47; Jeremiah 50, 51; and Zechariah 5:5-11.

F. Preservation of a Remnant (two-thirds of the Jews will perish, but a remnant will be preserved). Isaiah 26:20-21; Jeremiah 30:7; Daniel 12:1; and Zechariah 13:7-9.

IV. The Return of Jesus

A. The Circumstances: Israel under Attack
Isaiah 29:5-8; Isaiah 31:4-5; and Zechariah 14:1-2.

B. The Nature of the Return

1) The Lord's return is certain.
Habakkuk 2:2-4. (See Hebrews 10:36-38.)

2) The Lord's return will be visible.
Isaiah 30:19-20; Isaiah 35:2; Isaiah 60:2; and Zechariah 12:10.

3) The "Holy Ones" (the Redeemed) will come with the Lord.
Zechariah 14:5.

4) The Lord returns in glory.
Isaiah 63:1 and Habakkuk 3:3-4.

5) The Lord returns in wrath.
1 Samuel 2:10; 2 Samuel 22:8-16; Isaiah 13:9-13; Isaiah 26:20-21; Isaiah 30:27-28; Isaiah 34:1-4; Isaiah 59:15b-19; Isaiah 61:2b; Isaiah 63:1-6; Isaiah 66:15-16; Jeremiah 23:19-20; Jeremiah 25:30-31; Jeremiah 30:23-24; Amos 5:18-20; Nahum 1:2-3, 6; Habakkuk 3:6-15; and Zephaniah 1:14-18.

6) The Lord returns as a deliverer.
2 Samuel 22:7-20, 47-49; Isaiah 29:5-8; Isaiah 31:4-5; Isaiah 59:19-20; and Zechariah 14:1-2.

7) The Lord returns as a judge.
1 Samuel 2:10; 1 Chronicles 16:33; and Isaiah 33:22.

8) The Lord returns as a king.
Isaiah 33:22; Isaiah 45:23; Daniel 7:13-14; Micah 4:7; Zechariah 6:13; and Zechariah 14:9.

C. The Location of the Return: The Mount of Olives in Jerusalem
Zechariah 14:4. (See also: Isaiah 31:4; Isaiah 64:1; Micah 1:3-4; and Nahum 1:5-6.)

D. The Timing of the Return: "After Two Days" (2,000 years — see Psalm 90:4)
Hosea 5:15 - 6:2.

E. Nature's Response to the Return: Cataclysm
Isaiah 24:17-20; Isaiah 60:2; Jeremiah 4:23-28; Joel 2:30-31; Joel 3:14-15; Micah 1:3-4; Habakkuk 3:6-15; Zephaniah 1:14-15; and Zechariah 14:4-11.

F. The Results of the Return

1) The defeat of the Antichrist.
Isaiah 10:12-19; Isaiah 11:4; Isaiah 14:12-17; Isaiah 24:21-22; Isaiah 26:21 - 27:1; Isaiah 30:27-28; Isaiah 41:11-13; Isaiah 63:1-6; Isaiah 66:15-16; Daniel 7:11, 26; Daniel 11:45; Joel 3:12-16; Habakkuk 3:12-15; and Zechariah 14:3, 12-15.

2) Salvation of a Jewish remnant.
Isaiah 10:20-22; Isaiah 24:14-16; Isaiah 25:9; Isaiah 30:19-20; Isaiah 43:1-3; Isaiah 54:5-10; Isaiah 59:20; Isaiah 61:10; Jeremiah 4:27; Jeremiah 30:7; Jeremiah 31:1-7, 31-34; Jeremiah 33:6-8; Jeremiah 50:20; Ezekiel 6:8-10; Ezekiel 11:19-20; Ezekiel 20:42-44; Ezekiel 34:30-31; Ezekiel 36:25-28, 33; Ezekiel 37:14, 23; Ezekiel 39:28-29; Daniel 12:1; Hosea 2:14-20; Hosea 3:5; Hosea 5:15 - 6:2; Hosea 14:4-7; Joel 2:32; Obadiah 17; Micah 7:9, 18-20; Habakkuk 3:2b, 13; Zephaniah 2:3; Zephaniah 3:12-13; Zechariah 3:8-9; Zechariah 10:6, 8-9; Zechariah 12:10; and Zechariah 13:1, 9.

3) Renovation of the heavens and earth.
Isaiah 65:17.

V. The Post-Tribulation Period
(The interregnum of 75 days between the reign of the Antichrist and the formal beginning of the reign of Jesus Christ — see Daniel 12:11-12. For an explanatory discussion of this period of time, see page 54.)

A. Satan is Bound
Isaiah 24:21-22.

B. The Old Testament Saints are Resurrected and Glorified
Isaiah 26:19; Daniel 12:2; Hosea 6:2; and Hosea 13:14.

C. The Living Gentiles are Judged
(The New Testament indicates that the unrighteous will be consigned to death. Only the righteous who are alive at the end of the Tribulation will enter the Kingdom in the flesh.)
Isaiah 2:4; Isaiah 11:4-5; Joel 3:1-2, 12; and Micah 4:3.

D. The Living Jews are Judged and the Righteous Remnant is Gathered to Israel

1) The judgment.
Jeremiah 50:20 and Ezekiel 20:33-38, 42-43.

2) The gathering.
Isaiah 14:1-2; Isaiah 27:12-13; Isaiah 49:18-22; Isaiah 51:11; Jeremiah 3:12-14, 18; Jeremiah 23:3; Jeremiah 31:7-10; Jeremiah 32:37-41; Jeremiah 50:4-5, 19-20; Ezekiel 20:41-44; Ezekiel 28:25; Ezekiel 34:11-16; Ezekiel 37:21-23; Ezekiel 39:25-27; Hosea 2:14-15; Hosea 3:5; Hosea 11:10-11; Micah 2:12-13; Zephaniah 3:20; Zechariah 8:7-8; and Zechariah 10:6, 8-10.

VI. The Millennium

A. Jesus Reigns!

1) The fact of the reign.
1 Chronicles 17:11-14; Isaiah 9:6-7; Isaiah 24:23; Isaiah 28:5-6; Isaiah 32:1; Isaiah 33:17, 20-22; Isaiah 45:21-25; Isaiah 49:7; Isaiah 52:13-15; Jeremiah 23:5; Jeremiah 33:15; Ezekiel 43:7; Daniel 2:44-45; Daniel 7:13-14; Joel 3:17, 21; Obadiah 21; Micah 4:7; Micah 5:4; Zephaniah 3:14-17; Haggai 2:20-23 (Zerubbabel is a type of Christ); Zechariah 6:12-13 (Joshua is a type of Christ); Zechariah 9:10b; and Zechariah 14:9.

2) The nature of the reign.

a) World-wide.
Isaiah 2:2; Isaiah 4:7; Micah 4:1; Micah 5:4; and Zechariah 14:9.

b) Peaceful.
2 Samuel 7:10-11; Isaiah 2:4; Isaiah 9:7; Isaiah 32:17-18; Isaiah 60:18; Jeremiah 23:6; Jeremiah 30:8; Jeremiah 33:16; Ezekiel 28:25-26; Ezekiel 34:25-31; Hosea 2:18; Amos 9:15; Micah 4:3-4; Zechariah 2:4-5; Zechariah 8:12; and Zechariah 14:11.

c) Righteousness and justice abound.
2 Samuel 23:2-5; Isaiah 9:7; Isaiah 11:3b-5, 9; Isaiah 28:5-6; Isaiah 32:1-2, 15-18; Isaiah 33:5-6; Isaiah 42:1-4; Isaiah 61:8-9, 11; Jeremiah 23:5; Jeremiah 33:15; Hosea 2:19; and Habakkuk 2:14.

3) Political characteristics.

a) Throne in Jerusalem.
2 Samuel 7:10, 16; Isaiah 2:3; Jeremiah 3:17; Ezekiel 43:7; Joel 3:17, 21; Zechariah 2:12; and Zechariah 8:3.

b) Theocratic form of government.
(Combination of religious and political rule, characterized by nurturing care and discipline.) Isaiah 2:3; Isaiah 9:6-7; Isaiah 22:20-24 (Eliakim is a type of Christ); Isaiah 33:17, 20-22; Isaiah 40:10-11; Isaiah 45:21-25; Ezekiel 34:11-16; Micah 4:2; and Zechariah 6:12-13.

c) Saints reign with the Lord.
1 Samuel 2:8; Isaiah 32:1; Jeremiah 30:21; and Daniel 7:18, 27.

d) David reigns as king of Israel. (Jesus reigns as king of the world.)
Isaiah 55:3-4; Jeremiah 30:9; Ezekiel 34:23-24; Ezekiel 37:24-25; and Hosea 3:5.

e) Israel restored as the prime nation of the world.
2 Samuel 7:10; 2 Samuel 22:44-49; 1 Chronicles 17:22-24; Isaiah 2:2-3; Isaiah 49:22-23; Isaiah 60:1-7, 10-16; Isaiah 61:5-7; Isaiah 62:1-4; Isaiah 66:10-12; Jeremiah 4:1-2; Jeremiah 33:25-26; Ezekiel 36:15; Joel 2:26-27; Amos 9:11-12; Micah 4:1-2; Zephaniah 3:19-20; Zechariah 8:22-23; and Malachi 3:12.

4) Spiritual characteristics.

a) The glory and holiness of the Lord is manifested.
Isaiah 24:23; Isaiah 35:2; Isaiah 40:5; Isaiah 52:13, 15; Isaiah 60:21; Isaiah 61:3; Isaiah 66:18-19; Ezekiel 20:41; Ezekiel 28:25; Ezekiel 36:23; Ezekiel 39:21; and Habakkuk 2:14.

b) Israel is given a new covenant of peace.
Isaiah 42:6-7; Isaiah 49:8 (Jesus is the new covenant); Isaiah 54:10; Isaiah 55:3; Isaiah 59:21; Isaiah 61:8; Jeremiah 31:31-34; Jeremiah 32:40; Jeremiah 50:5; Ezekiel 16:60-63; Ezekiel 34:25; Ezekiel 37:26; and Hosea 2:18.

c) Israel is tutored spiritually by glorified Saints.
Jeremiah 3:15 and Jeremiah 23:4.

d) The Temple is rebuilt and a memorial sacrifice system is instituted.
Isaiah 56:7; Isaiah 60:7b, 13; Jeremiah 30:18; Jeremiah 33:18; Ezekiel 40-48; Ezekiel 37:26-28; Ezekiel 47:1; Ezekiel 48:8-10; Haggai 2:7-9; Zechariah 6:12-13, 15; Zechariah 14:16-20. (Note: No Ark is restored to the Holy of Holies because Jesus is our Ark — see Jeremiah 3:16.)

e) The Levitical priesthood is restored. (But only the sons of Zadok are allowed to minister to the altar.) Jeremiah 33:18-22; Ezekiel 40:46; Ezekiel 43:19; and Ezekiel 44:15.

f) Jesus serves as high priest (as well as king).
Zechariah 6:13.

g) David, "the prince," serves as worship leader.
Jeremiah 30:9, 21; Ezekiel 34:22-24; Ezekiel 37:24-25; Ezekiel 45:16-17, 21-25; Ezekiel 46:1-3; and Hosea 3:5.

h) Jerusalem is the center of world worship of Jesus.
Isaiah 2:2-3; Isaiah 35:8-10; Isaiah 56:6-8; Isaiah 66:18, 20; Jeremiah 3:17; Jeremiah 16:19-21; Ezekiel 40-48; Micah 4:1-2; Zechariah 8:20-22; and Zechariah 14:16.

i) The Shekinah glory of God hovers over Jerusalem.
Isaiah 4:5-6 and Isaiah 60:1-3.

j) The Holy Spirit is poured out.
Isaiah 32:15; Isaiah 44:3; Ezekiel 11:19; Ezekiel 36:27; Ezekiel 37:14; Ezekiel 39:29; Joel 2:28-29; and Zechariah 12:10.

k) The nations are evangelized.
Isaiah 11:9; Isaiah 66:19; and Zechariah 2:11.

l) The feasts of Passover and Tabernacles are observed by all peoples.
Ezekiel 45:21-25; and Zechariah 14:16-17.

m) Arabs and Jews unite in worship of God.
Isaiah 19:19-25 and Isaiah 45:14.

n) Holiness abounds.
Isaiah 4:2-4; Isaiah 11:9; Isaiah 60:21; Isaiah 62:12; Zechariah 13:2; and Zechariah 14:20.

o) An attitude of joy and praise prevails.
1 Chronicles 16:23-34; Isaiah 12; Isaiah 26:1-4; Isaiah 35:10; Isaiah 52:7-10; Isaiah 55:12; Isaiah 61:2b-3; Isaiah 65:18-19; Isaiah 66:13-14; Jeremiah 30:19; Jeremiah 31:3-6, 11-14; Jeremiah 33:9-11; Zephaniah 3:14-15; Zechariah 8:4-5; Zechariah 10:7; and Malachi 4:2.

B. Redemption of Nature and the Land

1) The topography of the area is radically changed.
Isaiah 35:1-2, 6b-7; Isaiah 40:3-5; Isaiah 41:18-20; Ezekiel 47:1-12; and Zechariah 14:10.

2) There is a reblossoming of the land (abundance of nature).
Isaiah 4:2; Isaiah 25:6; Isaiah 30:23-26; Isaiah 62:3-4; Isaiah 65:10; Ezekiel 34-36; Ezekiel 34:26-29; Ezekiel 36:30; Joel 2:24-26; Joel 3:18; Amos 9:13-14; Zechariah 8:12; and Malachi 3:11.

3) Nature is reconciled in peace.
    Isaiah 11:6-9; Isaiah 65:25; Ezekiel 34:25-29; and Hosea 2:18.

4) Ruins are rebuilt.
    Isaiah 58:12; Isaiah 61:4; Ezekiel 36:10, 33, 35; and Amos 9:14.

5) Jerusalem is rebuilt, enlarged and renamed "Yahweh-Shammah" (meaning "The Lord is There"). Isaiah 44:28 (Cyrus is a type of Christ); Isaiah 62:1-3; Jeremiah 3:17; Jeremiah 30:18; Jeremiah 31:38-40; Ezekiel 48:15-19, 30-35; Joel 3:17, 20. Zechariah 1:16-17; Zechariah 2:12; and Zechariah 14:11.

6) Fresh waters flow from Jerusalem.
    Ezekiel 47:1-12; Joel 3:18; and Zechariah 14:8.

7) The Dead Sea comes alive.
    Ezekiel 47:7-9 and Zechariah 14:8.

8) The land of Israel is enlarged and divided into east-west sections among the tribes.
    Ezekiel 47:13-23 and Ezekiel 48:1-29.

9) A highway is constructed uniting all of the Middle East.
    Isaiah 11:16; Isaiah 19:23; Isaiah 35:8; Isaiah 40:3; and Isaiah 62:10.

C. Life Enriched

1) The life span of Man is extended.
    Isaiah 33:24; Isaiah 65:19-22; and Zechariah 8:4.

2) Disease is curtailed.
    Isaiah 33:24; Isaiah 35:5-6; and Isaiah 65:23.

3) Healing is provided for mind and body.
    Isaiah 29:18-19; Isaiah 32:3-4; Isaiah 35:5-6; and Malachi 4:2.

4) Minds are purged of evil memories.
    Isaiah 65:16-17.

5) There is a rapid increase in population.
    Jeremiah 3:16; Jeremiah 30:19; Jeremiah 33:22; Ezekiel 36:10-11; and Ezekiel 37:26.

6) Language unity is restored.
    Zephaniah 3:9.

7) There is redemption of all labor.
    Isaiah 65:23.

8) There is great prosperity.
    Micah 4:4; Zechariah 1:17; and Zechariah 9:12.

VII. The Last Rebellion — The Battle of Gog and Magog at the End of the Millennium
(Revelation 20:7-10)

   A. The Lord Triumphs with Fire.
       Isaiah 66:15-16.

   B. The Judgment of the Unjust.
       1 Samuel 2:9 and Daniel 12:2.

   C. The Unrighteous are Cast into Hell (the "lake of fire" of Revelation 20:14).
       2 Samuel 23:6-7; Isaiah 66:24; and Daniel 12:2.

VIII. The Eternal State

   A. Provision of New Heavens and Earth
       Isaiah 66:22.

   B. The Lord is Present as the Light
       Isaiah 60:19-21.

   C. Death is Eliminated
       Isaiah 25:8.

   D. The Righteous are Rewarded

       1) All receive eternal life.
           Daniel 12:2.

       2) Some receive special rewards.
           Daniel 12:3.

D. THE PSALMS

1. INTRODUCTION

The Psalms are filled with prophetic references to Jesus, pertaining to both of His advents. Some are direct and clear. Others are indirect and subtle.

Messianic Psalms

Most scholars acknowledge that sixteen of the Psalms are distinctly Messianic in nature. They are listed below in figure 5.

All but three of these Psalms are directly quoted in the New Testament and applied to Christ. The three not quoted are Psalm 24, Psalm 72, and Psalm 89. The most frequently quoted is Psalm 110. It is mentioned a total

---

Figure 5

Listing of Generally Recognized Messianic Psalms with Examples of Prophetic Passages

Psalm 2 —	"You are My Son, today I have begotten You."	— The incarnation
	"I will surely give the nations as Your inheritance . . ."	— The reign of Jesus
Psalm 8 —	"You have made him [the Son of Man] a little lower . . ."	— The incarnation
Psalm 16 —	"You will not abandon my soul to Sheol . . ."	— The resurrection
Psalm 22 —	"My God, my God, why have You forsaken me?"	— The crucifixion
	"All the families of the nations will worship before You."	— The millennium
Psalm 24 —	"[Open] O gates . . . that the King of glory may come in."	— The second coming
Psalm 40 —	"Be pleased, O Lord to deliver me . . ."	— The crucifixion
Psalm 41 —	"Even my close friend, in whom I trusted . . ."	— The betrayal
Psalm 45 —	"She [the bride] will be led to the King . . ."	— The rapture
Psalm 68 —	"Let God arise, let His enemies be scattered . . ."	— The second coming
	"You have ascended on high . . ."	— The ascension
Psalm 69 —	"They gave me gall for my food and for my thirst . . ."	— The crucifixion
	"For God will save Zion and build the cities of Judah . . ."	— Salvation of Israel
Psalm 72 —	"Give the king Your judgments, O God . . ."	— The reign of Jesus
Psalm 89 —	"I shall make My first-born the highest of the kings . . ."	— The reign of Jesus
Psalm 91 —	"I will deliver him; I will set him securely on high . . ."	— The resurrection
Psalm 102 —	"Nations [and kings] will fear the name of the Lord . . ."	— The reign of Jesus
Psalm 110 —	"The Lord says to my Lord, 'Sit at My right hand . . .'"	— The ascension
	"The Lord will stretch forth Your strong scepter from Zion."	— The reign of Jesus
	"He will shatter kings in the day of His wrath."	— The second coming
Psalm 118 —	"The stone which the builders rejected has become . . ."	— The resurrection
	— "Blessed is the one who comes in the name of the Lord."	— The triumphal entry

Figure 6

Prophetic Passages from the Messianic Psalms
Arranged in Chronological Order

A. The First Coming

1)	Psalm 8:4-5; 40:6-10	— The Incarnation
2)	Psalm 91:9-13	— The Temptation
3)	Psalm 8:2; 118:25-26	— The Triumphal Entry
4)	Psalm 69:1-19	— The Gethsemane Agony
5)	Psalm 41:9	— The Betrayal
6)	Psalm 22:1-21; 40:13-17; 69:20-21	— The Crucifixion
7)	Psalm 16:8-11; 22:19-24; 91:11-16; 118:22	— The Resurrection
8)	Psalm 68:18; 110:1	— The Ascension
9)	Psalm 118:22	— The Church

B. The Second Coming

1)	Psalm 45:1-17	— The Rapture and the Marriage Feast
2)	Psalm 24:7-10	— The Return of the King of Glory
3)	Psalm 68:1-3; 110:5	— The Pouring Out of God's Wrath
4)	Psalm 2:4-9; 72:1-4; 89:19-29; 102:15; 110:2	— The King Reigns from Mt. Zion
5)	Psalm 110:1-7	— The King is a Priest and Judge
6)	Psalm 2:8; 8:3-9; 22:27-29	— The Dominion of the King
7)	Psalm 69:35-36; 102:12-22	— The Salvation and Restoration of Israel
8)	Psalm 22:25-31; 72:1-19	— The Millennium
9)	Psalm 89:4,27-29,36-37	— The Eternal Nature of the Reign

of fourteen times in the New Testament, more than any other Old Testament passage. Three other of these Messianic Psalms are mentioned frequently in the New Testament. They are Psalms 2 and 69, mentioned seven times each, and Psalm 118 which is cited a total of six times.

Together, these sixteen Messianic Psalms present a panoramic survey of the First and Second Comings of Jesus. Figure 6 presents passages from these sixteen psalms arranged in chronological order according to the events in the life of Jesus.

Other Messianic Psalms

The prophecies in the Psalms are by no means limited to the 16 acknowledged Mes-

sianic Psalms which are referenced above. I would add the following 17 Psalms to the list as ones that are obviously Messianic in nature, relating to the Lord's Second Coming:

1) Psalms 18 and 21— Contain vivid and detailed descriptions of the Lord's return in wrath. (Psalm 18:7-19 and Psalm 21:8-13)

2) Psalm 46 — Pictures the exalted Lord in the midst of Jerusalem following His triumphant return.

3) Psalm 47 — A song of joy celebrating the Lord's reign as King of kings.

4) Psalm 48 —The beauty of millennial Jerusalem.

5) Psalm 76 — A description of the battle of

Armageddon.

6) Psalms 96, 97, 98, 99 — Songs of joy celebrating the Lord's reign over the nations.

7) Psalms 145, 146, 147, 148, 149, 150 — Praise songs celebrating the glory, majesty, and goodness of the Lord's reign.

The addition of these 13 Psalms gives us a total of 33 Messianic Psalms. But even these 33 do not exhaust the rich treasure of prophetic material that is contained in the Psalms. In fact, the fundamental prophetic theme of the Psalms is not even reflected in any of the Messianic Psalms thus far identified.

Prophetic Themes

The basic prophetic focus of the Psalms is the suffering of the Jews during the Tribulation. From Psalm 3 through Psalm 144, there are 59 prayers for deliverance from tribulation. Twelve entire Psalms (80, 82, 88, 90, 120, 126, 129, 137, & 141-144) are devoted to earnest cries for deliverance from intense suffering.

Some might object to classifying these passages as prophetic in nature, arguing that they are simply the prayers of David and others who cried out to God in the midst of desperate situations. But some of the prayers are definitely national in nature (for example, Psalms 80 and 83). Others describe situations so horrible that they seem to point to the Great Tribulation for their fulfillment (see Psalms 14, 60, and 94).

As for the prayers that are definitely personal in nature, keep in mind that such utterances can have profound prophetic significance. The classic example is Psalm 22 where David in a moment of desperation cried out, "My God, my God, why have You forsaken me?" This was a personal prayer of David's, yet it was prophetic of the incredible agony that Jesus would suffer on the Cross when the sins of Mankind were placed upon Him and His perfect communion with His Father was broken for the first time. David's words became the Lord's words as He suffered on the Cross.

Likewise, I have no doubt that the Jews will turn to the Psalms in the midst of the Great Tribulation and pray these very prayers to God for their deliverance from God's wrath and the wrath of the Antichrist. Imagine yourself as a Jew in the Tribulation, hated by the nations and hunted like an animal by the Antichrist and his forces, and then read Psalm 88.

Statements of Faith, Rejoicing and Thanksgiving

Many of these heart-wrenching prayers are interspersed with triumphant statements of faith in God, as if the one crying out so desperately is trying to reassure himself that God is listening and will answer. Psalm 68:19 is typical:

> Blessed be the Lord,
> Who daily bears our burden,
> The God who is our salvation.
> God is to us a God of deliverance;
> And to God the Lord belongs escape
>   from death.

There are 46 such affirmations of faith contained in the prayers for deliverance. I can imagine the hard pressed Jews reading, memorizing, and reciting these statements during the darkest days of the Tribulation. Keep in mind, the prophet Zechariah says that two-thirds of the Jews will be destroyed during those terrible years (Zechariah 13:8).

Another repetitive theme of the Psalms is rejoicing and thanksgiving for the Lord's deliverance. Take Psalm 66 for example. It is an emotional and uninhibited song of praise for the national deliverance of Israel. You can imagine the leaping and clapping and dancing of the Jewish Remnant as you read the opening lines: "Shout joyfully to God, all the earth; sing the glory of His name; make His praise glorious!"

Sometimes a single Psalm will contain all three of these prophetic themes: 1) A cry for deliverance; 2) A statement of faith; and 3) A song of praise for God's delivering response. Psalm 54 is a good example of the combination of these themes:

1) The Cry for Deliverance — "Save me, O God, by Your name, and vindicate me by Your power. Hear my prayer, O God; give ear to the words of my mouth. For strangers have risen against me, and violent men have sought my life; they have not set God before them." (vs. 1-3)

2) The Expression of Faith — "Behold, God is my helper; the Lord is the sustainer of my soul. He will recompense the evil to my foes; destroy them in Your faithfulness." (vs. 4-5)

3) Praise for Deliverance — "Willingly I will sacrifice to You; I will give thanks to Your name, O Lord, for it is good. For He has delivered me from all trouble; and my eye has looked with satisfaction upon my enemies." (vs. 6-7)

Prophetic Units

A fascinating aspect of the Psalms is that they contain clusters of prophecies that relate to each other. The best known of these clusters is the prophetic trilogy of Psalms 22, 23, and 24.

Psalm 22 pictures Jesus in agony on the Cross. In Psalm 23 He is our resurrected High Priest, shepherding His flock through the power of His Spirit. In Psalm 24, He is the King of Glory who has returned to Jerusalem to reign over the nations. See figure 7 below.

Figure 7

A Prophetic Trilogy from the Psalms

Psalm 22	Psalm 23	Psalm 24
1) Suffering Savior	1) Ministering High Priest	1) Reigning King of Glory
2) First Advent	2) Spirit Advent	2) Second Advent
3) Redeemer	3) Anointer	3) Ruler
4) Good Shepherd "I am the good shepherd; the good shepherd lays down His life for the sheep." (John 10:11)	4) Great Shepherd "The God of peace ...brought up from the dead the great Shepherd of the sheep . . . even Jesus our Lord." (Hebrews 13:20)	4) Chief Shepherd "And when the Chief Shepherd appears, you will receive the unfading crown of glory." (1 Peter 5:4)

Other significant prophetic clusters in the Psalms are listed below:

A. Psalms 45-48
    1) Psalms 45   — The Rapture
    2) Psalms 46   — The Second Coming
    3) Psalms 47   — Hallelujah! Jesus Reigns!
    4) Psalms 48   — The Glory of Millennial Jerusalem

B.　Psalms 52-54
1)　Psalm 52　　　— The Fate of the Antichrist
2)　Psalm 53　　　— The Fate of the Ungodly
3)　Psalm 54　　　— The Fate of the Godly

C.　Psalms 65-67
1)　Psalm 65　　　— Praise for the Millennial Bounty of Nature
2)　Psalm 66　　　— Praise for the Jew's Deliverance
3)　Psalm 67　　　— Praise for God's Equitable Judgment of the Nations

D.　Psalms 109-111
1)　Psalm 109　　— Prayer for the Destruction of the Antichrist
2)　Psalm 110　　— Jesus Triumphs and Reigns as King and Priest
3)　Psalm 111　　— Praise to the Lord for His Faithfulness in Keeping His Covenant Promises

E.　Clusters of the Major Prophetic Themes
1)　Psalms 3-7　　　— Cries for Deliverance
2)　Psalms 103-105　— Expressions of Faith
3)　Psalms 141-144　— Praises for Deliverance
4)　Psalms 95-99　　— Celebrations of the Lord's Reign
5)　Psalms 145-150　— Praises of the King of Kings

Chronological Aspects

A popular theory in the late 20th Century theorized that the Psalms contained a chronological code. This theory was spelled out in detail by J. R. Church in his book, *Hidden Prophecies in the Psalms* (1986). The thesis was that since the book of Psalms is the 19th book of the Old Testament, it represents the 1900's, and thus Psalm 1 is prophetic of 1901, Psalm 2 of 1902, and so on. Psalms 88-94 were viewed in this interpretation as a picture of the Tribulation Period, corresponding to the years 1988-1994.

The theory was very unconvincing to me. First, it smacked of Kabalism, a form of Jewish mysticism that claims the real message of Scripture is encoded below the surface words. But a greater problem is that it did not line up with historical events.

For example, there is nothing in Psalm 48 that is prophetic of the re-establishment of the State of Israel in 1948. The Psalm is all about the beauty of Jerusalem. After the dust settled in the 1948 War of Liberation, Jerusalem was not even a part of the newly established Jewish State! The Jews did not re-occupy the city of Jerusalem until the Six Day War of 1967, yet Psalm 67 does not even mention Jerusalem.

A further problem for this theory of interpretation was presented by the fact that the Rapture of the Church is clearly portrayed in Psalm 45 where the Bride is pictured as being led to the Bridegroom-King. Yet, the Rapture did not occur in 1945. Also, Psalm 93 portrays the reign of the Lord — *before* the Tribulation was supposed to end in 1994!

Of course, with the passage of time, this once popular chronological theory has been completely disproved. ✤

2. AN OUTLINE OF SECOND ADVENT PROPHECIES IN THE PSALMS

I.   The Rapture (See discussion on pages 53-54.)

The Bride (the Church) is led to the Bridegroom (King Jesus) for the   Psalm 45
marriage feast. (See Revelation 19:6-9 for details about the feast.)

> "The King's daughter is all glorious within;
> Her clothing is interwoven with gold.
> She will be led to the King in embroidered work;
> The virgins, her companions, who follow her will be brought to You.
> They will be led forth in gladness and rejoicing;
> They will enter into the King's palace." (vs. 13-15 — For similar
>   imagery, see the Song of Solomon.)

II. The Tribulation

A. The Atmosphere of Ungodliness   Psalm 14

> "The fool has said in his heart, 'There is no God.'
> They are corrupt, they have committed abominable deeds;
> There is no one who does good . . .
> They have all turned aside, together they have become corrupt . . ."
> (vs. 1 and 3. See also Psalm 53:1-3.)

B. The Wrath of God

1) Poured out on all nations.   Psalm 75

> "For a cup is in the hand of the Lord, and the wine foams;
> It is well mixed, and He pours out this;
> Surely all the wicked of the earth must drain and drink down
>   its dregs." (vs. 8. See also Revelation 16.)

2) Poured out on Israel in particular.   Psalm 60

> "O God . . .
> You have made the land quake, You have split it open;
> Heal its breaches, for it totters.
> You have made Your people experience hardship;
> You have given us wine to drink that makes us stagger."
> (vs. 1-3)

C. The Antichrist

   1) The treachery of the Antichrist: A friend turns enemy.   Psalm 55

   "For it is not an enemy who reproaches me,
   Then I could bear it;
   Nor is it one who hates me who has exalted himself against me,
   Then I could hide myself from him.
   But it is you, a man my equal,
   My companion and my familiar friend . . .
   He has put forth his hands against those who were at peace
       with him;
   He has violated his covenant.
   His speech was smoother than butter,
   But his heart was war . . ." (vs. 12-13, 20-21)

   [Note: The New Testament applies this passage to Judas, but keep in
   mind that Judas is a type of the Antichrist. Like Judas who befriended
   Jesus, the Antichrist will appear first as a friend of Israel and then will
   double cross the Jews and attempt to exterminate them. See Daniel
   9:27 and Revelation 12:13-17.]

   2) The deceitful and prideful nature of the Antichrist.

      a) "For the wicked boasts of his heart's desire . . .   Psalm 10
          His mouth is full of curses and deceit and oppression;
          Under his tongue is mischief and wickedness."
          (vs. 3 and 7)

      b) "Why do you boast in evil, O mighty man? . . .   Psalm 52
          Your tongue devises destruction,
          Like a sharp razor, O worker of deceit.
          You love evil more than good,
          Falsehood more than speaking what is right.
          You love all words that devour,
          O deceitful tongue." (vs. 1-4. See also Daniel 11:36.)

   3) The wrath of the Antichrist and his forces.

      a) "[The wicked] crush Your people, O Lord,   Psalm 94
          And afflict Your heritage.
          They slay the widow and the stranger
          And murder the orphans." (vs. 5-6. See also Psalm 64:1-6.)

      b) "Help, Lord, for the godly man ceases to be,   Psalm 12
          For the faithful disappear from among the sons
              of men." (vs. 1)

4) The genocidal purpose of the Antichrist.   Psalm 83

"And those who hate You have exalted themselves.
They make shrewd plans against Your people,
And conspire together against Your treasured ones.
They have said, 'Come, and let us wipe them out as a nation,
That the name of Israel be remembered no more.'" (vs. 2-4)

D. The Nation of Israel

1) The Jews cry out to God for deliverance from wrath.

a) "Bow Your heavens, O Lord, and come down;   Psalm 144
   Touch the mountains [kingdoms], that they may smoke."
   (vs. 5)

b) "Keep me as the apple of the eye;   Psalm 17
   Hide me in the shadow of Your wings,
   From the wicked who despoil me,
   My deadly enemies who surround me." (vs. 8-9)

c) "Lord, How long will You look on?   Psalm 35
   Rescue my soul from their ravages,
   My only life from the lions." (vs. 17)

d) "O God, hasten to deliver me;   Psalm 70
   O Lord, hasten to my help!
   Let those be ashamed and humiliated
   Who seek my life." (vs. 1-2. See also Psalm 88)

e) "Rescue me, O my God, out of the hand of the wicked,   Psalm 71
   Out of the grasp of the wrongdoer and ruthless man,
   For you are my hope . . ." (vs. 4-5)

f) "O Lord God of hosts,   Psalm 80
   How long will You be angry with the prayer of
        Your people? . . .
   You make us an object of contention to our neighbors;
   And our enemies laugh among themselves.
   O God of hosts, restore us." (vs. 4-7. See also
   Psalm 44:14-15 and Psalm 31:9-11)

g) "As a shattering of my bones, my adversaries revile me,   Psalm 42
   While they say to me all day long, 'Where is your God?'"
   (vs. 10)

2) The Jews lament the destruction of Jerusalem and the Temple.

    a) "O God . . .   Psalm 74
       Remember . . . Mt. Zion, where You have dwelt . . .
       The enemy has damaged everything within the sanctuary.
       Your enemies have roared in the midst of Your
          meeting place . . ." (vs. 1-4. See also Lamentations.)

    b) "O God, the nations have invaded Your inheritance;   Psalm 79
       They have defiled Your holy temple;
       They have laid Jerusalem in ruins." (vs. 1)

3) The Jews pray for the destruction of the Antichrist.

    a) "Let his days be few . . .   Psalm 109
       Let his children be fatherless
       And his wife a widow . . .
       Let his posterity be cut off . . ." (vs. 8-9, 13, 15)

    b) "May the Lord cut off all flattering lips,   Psalm 12
       The tongue that speaks great things;
       Who have said, ' . . . who is Lord over us?'" (vs. 3-4)

4) The Jewish Remnant thanks God for compassionate Gentiles.   Psalm 41

    "How blessed is he who considers the helpless;
    The Lord will deliver him in a day of trouble.
    The Lord will protect him, and keep him alive,
    And he shall be called blessed upon the earth;
    And do not give him over to the desire of his enemies." (vs. 1-2)

5) The Jewish Remnant expresses its faith that God will deliver them.

    a) "My soul waits in silence for God only;   Psalm 62
       From Him is my salvation.
       He only is my rock and my salvation,
       My stronghold; I shall not be greatly shaken." (vs. 1-2)

    b) "So I will bless You as long as I live;   Psalm 63
       I will lift up my hands in Your name . . .
       But those who seek my life, to destroy it,
       Will go into the depths of the earth.
       They will be delivered over to the power of the sword;
       They will be a prey for foxes." (vs. 4, 9-10)

    c) "In You, O Lord, I have taken refuge . . .   Psalm 71
       Be to me a rock of habitation . . .
       Rescue me, O my God, out of the hands of the wicked,
       Out of the grasp of the wrongdoer and ruthless man,
       For You are my hope . . ." (vs. 1, 3-5)

      d) "For the Lord will not abandon His people,   Psalm 94
           Nor will He forsake His inheritance.
           For judgment will again be righteous . . ." (vs. 14-15)

6) God demands that the Jews repent.

      a) "'Now consider this, you who forget God,   Psalm 50
           Or I will tear you in pieces, and there be none to deliver.
           He who offers a sacrifice of thanksgiving honors Me;
           And to him who orders his way aright
           I shall show the salvation of God.'" (vs. 22-23)

      b) "'Hear, O My people, and I will admonish you . . .   Psalm 81
           Oh that My people would listen to Me,
           That Israel would walk in My ways!
           I would quickly subdue their enemies . . .'" (vs. 8, 13-14)

7) The Jewish Remnant repents.

      a) "I acknowledged my sin to You,   Psalm 32
           And my iniquity I did not hide;
           I said, 'I will confess my transgressions to the Lord;'
           And You forgave the guilt of my sin." (vs. 5)

      b) "For I am ready to fall,   Psalm 38
           And my sorrow is continually before me.
           For I confess my iniquity;
           I am full of anxiety because of my sin." (vs. 17-18.
           See also Psalm 39:7-13)

      c) "Be gracious to me, O God, according to Your loving-   Psalm 51
              kindness;
           According to the greatness of Your compassion blot out
              my transgressions.
           Wash me thoroughly from my iniquity,
           And cleanse me from my sin." (vs. 1-2)

           [Note: David's great prayer seeking forgiveness for his adultery will become the prayer of the Remnant as they seek forgiveness for their spiritual adultery.]

      d) "Search me, O God, and know my heart;   Psalm 139
           Try me and know my anxious thoughts;
           And see if there be any hurtful way in me,
           And lead me in the everlasting way." (vs. 23-24)

III. The Return of Jesus

A. The Nature of His Return

1) He returns in wrath.

a) "Your hand will find out all your enemies;   Psalm 21
   Your right hand will find out those who hate you.
   You will make them as a fiery oven in the time of
       your anger;
   The Lord will swallow them up in His wrath,
   And fire will devour them." (vs. 8-9)

b) "Then the earth shook and quaked;   Psalm 18
   And the foundations of the mountains were trembling
   And were shaken, because He was angry.
   Smoke went up out of His nostrils,
   And fire from His mouth devoured;
   Coals were kindled by it.
   He bowed the heavens also, and came down
   With thick darkness under His feet." (vs. 7-9. See also
   Psalm 76:3-9)

c) "Upon the wicked He will rain snares;   Psalm 11
   Fire and brimstone and burning wind will be the portion
       of their cup." (vs. 6)

2) He returns in wrath to judge Israel.   Psalm 50

"May our God come and not keep silence;
Fire devours before Him,
And it is very tempestuous around Him.
He summons the heavens above,
And the earth, to judge His people:
'Gather my godly ones to Me,
Those who have made a covenant with Me by sacrifice.'
And the heavens declare His righteousness,
For God Himself is judge." (vs. 3-6)

3) He returns in wrath as a righteous judge of the nations.

a) "The nations made an uproar, the kingdoms tottered;   Psalm 46
   He raised His voice, the earth melted.
   The Lord of hosts is with us . . .
   Come, behold the works of the Lord,
   Who has wrought desolations on the earth." (Vs. 6-8)

b) "He [the Lord] will shatter kings in the day of His wrath.   Psalm 110
He will judge among the nations,
He will fill them with corpses." (vs. 5-6)

c) "You have rebuked the nations,   Psalm 9
You have destroyed the wicked;
You have blotted out their name forever and ever."
(vs. 5-6)

d) "Then all the trees of the forest will sing with joy   Psalm 96
Before the Lord, for He is coming,
For He is coming to judge the earth.
He will judge the world in righteousness,
And the peoples in His faithfulness." (vs. 12-13)

4) He returns in majesty and glory.

a) "Lift up your heads, O gates,   Psalm 24
And be lifted up, O ancient doors,
That the King of glory may come in!
Who is the King of glory?
The Lord strong and mighty,
The Lord mighty in battle." (vs. 7-8)

b) "'Cease striving and know that I am God.   Psalm 46
I will be exalted among the nations, I will be exalted
in the earth.'
The Lord of hosts is with us;
The God of Jacob is our stronghold." (vs. 10-11)

B. The Consequences of the Lord's Return

1) The fate of the Antichrist.   Psalm 52

"Why do you boast in evil, O mighty man? . . .
But God will break you down forever;
He will snatch you up, and tear you away from your tent,
And uproot you from the land of the living.
The righteous will see and fear,
And will laugh at him, saying,
'Behold, the man who would not make God his refuge.
But trusted in the abundance of his riches
And was strong in his evil desire.'" (vs. 1, 5-7)

2) The fate of the ungodly.

a) "The wicked shall depart to Sheol,   Psalm 9
all the nations that forget God." (vs. 17 — RSV)

b) "Have those who work evil no understanding,   Psalm 53
  who eat up my people as they eat bread,
  and do not call upon God?
There they are, in great terror,
  in terror such as has not been!
For God will scatter the bones of the ungodly;
  they will be put to shame." (vs. 4-5 — RSV)

c) "But You, O Lord, are on high forever.   Psalm 92
For, behold . . . Your enemies will perish;
All who do iniquity will be scattered." (vs. 8-9. See also
Psalm 37:20, 28, 38; Psalm 49:10 and Psalm 73:17-20, 27)

3) The fate of the godly.

a) "Behold, God is my helper . . .   Psalm 54
He will recompense the evil to my foes . . .
Thanks to Your name, O Lord . . .
For He has delivered me from all trouble." (vs. 4-7)

b) "The righteous man will flourish like the palm tree . . .   Psalm 92
Planted in the house of the Lord,
They will flourish in the courts of our God . . .
To declare that the Lord is upright." (vs. 12-13, 15)

c) "For the Lord loves justice   Psalm 37
And does not forsake His godly ones;
They are preserved forever." (vs. 28)

4) The Jewish Remnant praises God for His deliverance.

a) "When the Lord restores His captive people,   Psalm 14
Jacob will rejoice, Israel will be glad." (vs. 7. See also Psalm
53:6)

b) "I will give thanks to the Lord with all my heart . . .   Psalm 9
For You have maintained my just cause;
You have sat on the throne judging righteously.
You have rebuked the nations, You have destroyed
  the wicked." (vs. 1, 4-5)

c) "The Lord lives, and blessed be my rock;   Psalm 18
And exalted be the God of my salvation,
The God who executes vengeance for me,
And subdues peoples under me.
He delivers me from my enemies." (vs. 46-48)

d) "I will extol You, O Lord, for You have lifted me up,   Psalm 30
   And have not let my enemies rejoice over me . . .
   You have turned for me my mourning into dancing . . ."
   (vs. 1, 11)

e) "I will bless the Lord at all times . . .   Psalm 34
   I sought the Lord, and He answered me,
   And delivered me from all my fears . . .
   This poor man cried, and the Lord heard him . . .
   The angel of the Lord encamps around those who
        fear Him,
   And rescues them." (vs. 1, 4, 6-7. See also Psalm 40:1-5.)

f) "O sing to the Lord a new song,   Psalm 98
   For He has done wonderful things,
   His right hand and His holy arm have gained the
        victory for Him.
   The Lord has made known His salvation;
   He has revealed His righteousness in the sight of the nations.
   He has remembered His lovingkindness and His faithfulness
        to the house of Israel;
   All the ends of the earth have seen the salvation of our God."
   (vs. 1-3)

g) "From heaven the Lord gazed upon the earth,   Psalm 102
   To hear the groaning of the prisoner,
   To set free those who were doomed to death,
   That men may tell of the name of the Lord in Zion
   And His praise in Jerusalem." (vs. 19-21. See also vs. 16-17)

h) "I love the Lord, because He hears   Psalm 116
   My voice and my supplications . . .
   The cords of death encompassed me
   And the terrors of Sheol came upon me;
   I found distress and sorrow.
   Then I called upon the name of the Lord:
   'O Lord, I beseech You, save my life!' . . .
   The Lord preserves the simple;
   I was brought low, and He saved me." (vs. 1, 3-4, 6)

i) "[The nations] pushed me violently so that I was falling,   Psalm 118
   But the Lord helped me.
   The Lord is my strength and song,
   And He has become my salvation." (vs. 13-14)

j) "'Had it not been for the Lord who was on our side,   Psalm 124
   Let Israel now say . . . 'When men rose up against us,
   Then they would have swallowed us alive' . . .

Blessed be the Lord,
Who has not given us to be torn by their teeth.
Our soul has escaped as a bird out of the snare of
    the trapper . . .
Our help is in the name of the Lord . . ." (vs. 1-2, 6-8)

5) The resurrection of the righteous Jews.

   a) "As for me, I shall behold Your face in righteousness;   Psalm 17
      I will be satisfied with Your likeness when I awake."
      (vs. 15. See also Psalm 49:15)

   b) "I would have despaired unless I had believed that I   Psalm 27
        would see the goodness of the Lord
      In the land of the living." (vs. 13. See also Job 19:26-27)

6) The righteous inherit the earth.   Psalm 37

   "The righteous will inherit the land,
   And dwell in it forever." (vs. 29. See also vs. 9, 11, 22, 34)

7) The Jews inherit the land of Israel.   Psalm 69

   "For God will save Zion and build the cities of Judah,
   That they may dwell there and possess it.
   And the descendants of His servants will inherit it,
   And those who love His name will dwell in it." (vs. 35-36)

IV. The Millennium

A. Jesus Reigns!

1) The fact of the Lord's reign.   Psalm 96

   "Say among the nations, 'The Lord reigns;
   Indeed, the world is firmly established, it will not be moved;
   He will judge the peoples with equity.'" (vs. 10)

2) The world-wide dominion of the Lord's reign.

   a) "Ask of Me, and I will surely give the nations as Your   Psalm 2
        inheritance,
      And the very ends of the earth as Your possession."
      (vs. 8. See also Psalm 86:9.)

   b) "Shout to God with the voice of joy.   Psalm 47
      For the Lord Most High is to be feared,
      A great King over all the earth." (vs. 1-2)

    c) "You have placed me as head of the nations;   Psalm 18
        A people whom I have not known serve me . . .
        Foreigners submit to me . . .
        Therefore I will give thanks to You among the nations,
          O Lord." (vs. 43-44, 49)

    d) "For the kingdom is the Lord's   Psalm 22
        And He rules over the nations." (vs. 28)

3) The Lord's reign extends over all kings — He is the King of kings.

    a) "'I also shall make him My first born,   Psalm 89
        The highest of the kings of the earth.'" (vs. 27)

    b) "So the nations will fear the name of the Lord   Psalm 102
        And all the kings of the earth Your glory." (vs. 15. See also
        Psalm 76:11-12)

    c) "All the kings of the earth will give thanks to You,   Psalm 138
          O Lord." (vs. 4)

4) The Lord shares His reign with the Saints.

    a) "In place of your fathers will be your sons;   Psalm 45
        You shall make them princes in all the earth." (vs. 16)

    b) "O clap your hands, all peoples;   Psalm 47
        Shout to God with the voice of joy.
        For the Lord Most High is to be feared,
        A great King over all the earth.
        He subdues peoples under us
        And nations under our feet." (vs. 1-3)

5) The Lord manifests His glory in His reign.

    a) "And You crown him [the son of man] with glory   Psalm 8
          and majesty!
        You make him to rule over the works of Your hands;
        You have put all things under his feet . . ." (vs. 5-6)

    b) "[The King's] glory is great through Your salvation,   Psalm 21
        Splendor and majesty You place upon him.
        For You make him most blessed forever." (vs. 5-6)

B. Prayers for the King's Reign

   1) That His reign will be everlasting.   Psalm 61

     "Prolong the life of the king;
       may his years endure to all generations!
     May he be enthroned forever before God;
       bid steadfast love and faithfulness watch over him!"
     (vs. 6-7 — RSV)

   2) That His reign will be characterized by justice, righteousness,   Psalm 72
      and compassion.

     "Give the king Your judgments, O God . . .
     May he judge Your people with righteousness
     And Your afflicted with justice . . .
     He will have compassion on the poor and needy,
     And the lives of the needy he will save." (vs. 1-2, 13)

   3) That His reign will be one of great bounty.   Psalm 144

     "Let our sons in their youth be as grown-up plants,
     And our daughters as corner pillars fashioned as for a palace;
     Let our garners be full, furnishing every kind of produce,
     And our flocks bring forth thousands and ten thousands
        in our fields;
     Let our cattle bear
     Without mishap and without loss . . ." (vs. 12-14)

C. The Unique Nature of the Lord's Reign — A theocracy in which   Psalm 110
   Jesus reigns as both King and Priest

   "The Lord will stretch forth Your strong scepter from Zion,
     saying,
  'Rule in the midst of Your enemies . . .
  You are a priest forever
  According to the order of Melchizedek.'" (vs. 2, 4)

D. The Beauty of the Lord's Reign

   1) The glory and majesty of the Lord's reign.

     a) They have seen Your procession, O God,   Psalm 68
        The procession of my God, my King, into the sanctuary . . .
        O God, You are awesome from Your sanctuary."
        (vs. 24, 35)

b) "The Lord reigns, He is clothed with majesty;   Psalm 93
The Lord has clothed and girded Himself with strength . . .
Holiness befits Your house,
O Lord, forevermore." (vs. 1, 5)

2) The glory of millennial Jerusalem.

a) "Great is the Lord, and greatly to be praised,   Psalm 48
In the city of our God, His holy mountain.
Beautiful in elevation, the joy of the whole earth,
Is Mount Zion in the far north,
The city of the great King." (vs. 1-2. See also Psalm 76:1-2)

b) "His foundation is in the holy mountains.   Psalm 87
The Lord loves the gates of Zion
More than all the other dwelling places of Jacob.
Glorious things are spoken of you,
O city of God." (vs. 1-3)

c) "A mountain of many peaks is the mountain of Bashan.   Psalm 68
Why do you look with envy, O mountains with many peaks,
At the mountain which God has desired for His abode?
Surely the Lord will dwell there [Zion] forever." (vs. 15-16)

d) "For the Lord has chosen Zion;   Psalm 132
He has desired it for His habitation.
'This is My resting place forever;
Here I will dwell, for I have desired it.
I will abundantly bless her provision . . .'" (vs. 13-15)

3) The glory of the millennial Temple.   Psalm 84

"How lovely are Your dwelling places,
O Lord of hosts!
My soul longed and even yearned for the courts of the Lord . . .
How blessed are those who dwell in Your house!
They are ever praising You." (vs. 1-2, 4)

E. The Righteousness of the Lord's Reign

1) The passion for the righteousness that will characterize the saints who
reign with Jesus.

a) "O Lord, who may abide in Your tent? . . .   Psalm 15
He who walks with integrity, and works righteousness,
And speaks truth in his heart.
He does not slander with his tongue,
Nor does evil to his neighbor . . ." (vs. 1-3. See also
Psalm 24:3-6)

b) "Let the words of my mouth and the meditation of my   Psalm 19
      heart
   Be acceptable in Your sight,
   O Lord, my rock and my Redeemer." (vs. 14)

c) "I will walk within my house in the integrity of my heart.   Psalm 101
   I will set no worthless thing before my eyes . . .
   A perverse heart shall depart from me;
   I will know no evil . . .
   My eyes shall be upon the faithful of the land, that they may
      dwell with me . . ." (vs. 2-4, 6. See also Psalm 141)

d) "I was glad when they said to me,   Psalm 122
   'Let us go to the house of the Lord.'" (vs. 1)

2) The glory of God's Word as the all-sufficient source of law and edu-
   cation.

   a) "How blessed is the man . . .   Psalm 1
      [Whose] delight is in the law of the Lord,
      And in His law he mediates day and night.
      He will be like a tree firmly planted by streams of water,
      Which yields its fruit in its season
      And its leaf does not wither;
      And in whatever he does, he prospers." (vs. 1-3)

   b) "The law of the Lord is perfect, restoring the soul;   Psalm 19
      The testimony of the Lord is sure, making wise the simple.
      The precepts of the Lord are right, rejoicing the heart;
      The commandment of the Lord is pure, enlightening
         the eyes." (vs. 7-8)

   c) "How blessed is the man who fears the Lord,   Psalm 112
      Who greatly delights in His commandments . . .
      Wealth and riches are in his house . . .
      He is gracious and compassionate and righteous . . .
      He will not fear evil tidings." (vs. 1-7. See also Proverbs
      13:13 and Ecclesiastes 12:13)

   d) "How blessed are those whose way is blameless,   Psalm 119
      Who walk in the law of the Lord.
      How blessed are those who observe His testimonies . . .
      Oh that my ways may be established
      To keep Your statutes!" (vs. 1-2, 5)

F. The Justice of the Lord's Reign

    1) "O Lord, You have heard the desire of the humble;   Psalm 10
        You will strengthen their heart, You will incline Your ear
        To vindicate the orphan and the oppressed . . ." (vs. 17-18.
        See also Psalm 68:5)

    2) "For He will deliver the needy when he cries for help,   Psalm 72
        The afflicted also, and him who has no helper.
        He will have compassion on the poor and needy,
        And the lives of the needy he will save.
        He will rescue their life from oppression and violence . . ."
        (vs. 12-14)

G. The Peace of the Lord's Reign

    1) "As the mountains surround Jerusalem,   Psalm 125
        So the Lord surrounds His people
        From this time forth and forever . . .
        Peace be upon Israel. (vs. 2, 5)

    2) "The Lord is your keeper;   Psalm 121
        The Lord is your shade on your right hand.
        The sun will not smite you by day,
        Nor the moon by night.
        The Lord will protect you from all evil;
        He will keep your soul.
        The Lord will guard your going out and your coming in
        From this time forth and forever." (vs. 5-8)

H. Spiritual Principles of the Lord's Reign

    1) Trust in God.

        a) "Unless the Lord builds the house,   Psalm 127
            They labor in vain who build it.
            Unless the Lord guards the city,
            The watch-man keeps awake in vain." (vs. 1. See also
            Proverbs 3:5-6; Proverbs 16:3; and Proverbs 19:21)

        b) "It is better to take refuge in the Lord   Psalm 118
            Than to trust in man." (vs. 8. See also Psalm 56:3-4, 9-11)

        c) "Some boast in chariots and some in horses,   Psalm 20
            But we will boast in the name of the Lord, our God." (vs. 7)

    2) Fear of God.   Psalm 128

       "How blessed is everyone who fears the Lord,
       Who walks in His ways.
       When you shall eat of the fruit of your hands,
       You will be happy." (vs. 1-2. See also Proverbs 1:7; Proverbs
       14:27 and Ecclesiastes 12:13)

    3) Brotherly Love.   Psalm 133

       "Behold, how good and pleasant it is
       For brothers to dwell together in unity!" (vs. 1)

I. The Atmosphere of Joy and Praise and Worship

    1) Celebration of the Lord as King of kings.   Psalm 95

       "O come let us sing for joy to the Lord,
       Let us shout joyfully to the rock of our salvation . . .
       For the Lord is a great God
       And a great King above all gods." (vs. 1, 3)

    2) Celebration of the Lord for the righteousness of His
       judgments.

       a) "Let the heavens be glad, and let the earth rejoice . . .   Psalm 96
          Before the Lord, for He is coming,
          For He is coming to judge the earth.
          He will judge the world in righteousness
          And the peoples in His faithfulness." (vs. 11, 13)

       b) "The Lord reigns; let the earth rejoice . . .   Psalm 97
          Righteousness and justice are the foundations of His
            throne." (vs. 1-2)

       c) "Shout joyfully to the Lord, all the earth . . .   Psalm 98
          Let the mountains sing together for joy
          Before the Lord, for He is coming to judge the earth;
          He will judge the world with righteousness
          And the peoples with equity." (vs. 4, 8-9)

    3) Praise for the Lord's holiness and justice.   Psalm 99

       "The Lord reigns, let the peoples tremble . . .
       Let them praise Your great and awesome name;
       Holy is He." (vs. 1, 3)

4) Praise for the Lord's love.

    a) "Shout joyfully to the Lord, all the earth . . .   Psalm 100
       Enter His gates with thanksgiving . . .
       For the Lord is good;
       His lovingkindness is everlasting . . ." (vs. 1, 4-5)

    b) "Praise the Lord, all nations . . .   Psalm 117
       For His lovingkindness is great toward us." (vs. 1-2)

    c) "Sing for joy in the Lord, O you righteous ones . . .   Psalm 33
       The earth is full of the lovingkindness of the Lord."
       (vs. 1, 5)

5) Praise for the Lord's grace and mercy.

    a) Praise the Lord! . . .   Psalm 113
       He raises the poor from the dust
       And lifts the needy from the ash heap,
       To make them sit with princes . . ." (vs. 1, 7-8)

    b) "The Lord is gracious and merciful;   Psalm 145
       Slow to anger and great in lovingkindness.
       The Lord is good to all,
       And His mercies are over all His works." (vs. 8-9)

6) Praise for the Lord's healing.   Psalm 146

"Praise the Lord! . . .
The Lord sets the prisoners free.
The Lord opens the eyes of the blind;
The Lord raises up those who are bowed down . . ."
(vs. 1, 7-8)

7) Praise for the bounty of the Millennium.   Psalm 65

"You visit the earth, and cause it to overflow;
You greatly enrich it . . .
You bless it with growth.
You have crowned the year with Your bounty. (vs. 9-11)

8) Joy and praise of the Jews for the Lord's blessings upon Israel.

    a) "Bless our God, O peoples,   Psalm 66
       And sound His praise abroad . . .
       For You have tried us, O God;
       You have refined us as silver is refined. . .
       We went through fire . . .
       Yet You brought us out into a place of abundance."
       (vs. 8, 10, 12)

    b) "Praise the Lord, O Jerusalem! . . .   Psalm 147
        He makes peace in your borders;
        He satisfies you with the finest of wheat . . .
        He has not dealt with any nation . . ." (vs. 12, 14, 20)

    c) "Praise the Lord! . . .   Psalm 111
        He has made known to His people the power of
           His works,
        In giving them the heritage of the nations." (vs. 1, 6)

9) Joy and praise of the Gentile nations for the Lord's equity.   Psalm 67

    "Let the peoples praise You, O God . . .
    For You will judge the peoples with uprightness
    And guide the nations on the earth." (vs. 3-4)

10) Joy and praise of the material universe for the Lord's   Psalm 148
    redemption.

    "Praise the Lord! . . .
    Praise the Lord from the heavens . . .
    Praise Him sun and moon;
    Praise Him, all stars of light!
    Praise the Lord from the earth
    Sea monsters and all deeps . . .
    Mountains and all hills;
    Fruit trees and all cedars;
    Beasts and all cattle;
    Creeping things and winged fowl . . .
    [For] He has lifted up a horn for His people . . ." (vs. 1, 3, 7,
    9-10, 14)

11) Worship of the Lord for who He is.

    a) "Behold, bless the Lord, all servants of the Lord . . .   Psalm 134
        He who made heaven and earth." (vs. 1, 3)

    b) "You who revere the Lord, bless the Lord.   Psalm 135
        Blessed be the Lord from Zion,
        Who dwells in Jerusalem." (vs. 20-21)

    c) "Give thanks to the Lord, for He is good;   Psalm 136
        For His lovingkindness is everlasting." (vs. 1)

    d) "Sing to the Lord a new song,   Psalm 149
        And His praise in the congregation of the godly ones . . .
        For the Lord takes pleasure in His people." (vs. 1, 4)

    e) "Praise the Lord!
        Praise God in His sanctuary;
        Praise Him in His mighty expanse.
        Praise Him for His mighty deeds;
        Praise Him according to His excellent greatness." (vs. 1-2)   Psalm 150

    f) "All the ends of the earth will remember and turn to
          the Lord,
        And all the families of the nations will worship
          before You." (vs. 27)   Psalm 22

    g) "Ascribe to the Lord glory and strength.
        Ascribe to the Lord the glory due to His name;
        Worship the Lord in holy array . . .
        Yes, the Lord sits as King forever." (vs. 1-2, 10)   Psalm 29

V. The Judgment of the Ungodly

A. The Ungodly Will Bow Their Knees Before the Lord.   Psalm 22

"All those who go down to the dust will bow before Him,
Even he who cannot keep his soul alive." (vs. 29)

B. The Ungodly Will be Condemned.

    1) "Therefore the wicked will not stand in the judgment,   Psalm 1
        Nor sinners in the assembly of the righteous.
        For the Lord knows the way of the righteous,
        But the way of the wicked will perish." (vs. 5-6. See also
        Ecclesiastes 12:14)

    2) "[The enemies of the Lord] add iniquity to their iniquity,   Psalm 69
        And may they not come into Your righteousness.
        May they be blotted out of the book of life
        And may they not be recorded with the righteous." (vs. 27-28)

VI. The Eternal State

A. The Heavens and Earth to be Renewed   Psalm 102

"Of old You founded the earth
And the heavens are the work of Your hands.
Even they will perish, but You endure;
And all of them will wear out like a garment;
Like clothing You will change them
And they will be changed." (vs. 25-26)

B. The Nature of the Lord's Reign

    1) The Lord will reign forever.

        a) "So I will establish his descendants forever   Psalm 89
           And his throne as the days of heaven." (vs. 29)

        b) "The Lord is King forever and ever."   Psalm 10
           (vs. 16. See also Psalm 145:13)

    2) The Lord will have dominion over all creation.   Psalm 8

      "You make him to rule over the works of Your hands;
      You have put all things under his feet . . ." (vs. 6)

C. Everlasting Characteristics of the Lord's Reign

    1) The eternal blessedness of the Saints.   Psalm 23

      "Surely goodness and lovingkindness will follow me all
        the days of my life,
      And I will dwell in the house of the Lord forever." (vs. 6)

    2) The eternal authority of God's Word.   Psalm 119

      "The sum of Your word is truth,
      And every one of Your righteous ordinances is everlasting."
      (vs. 160)

    3) The eternal love of God.   Psalm 136

      "Give thanks to the God of heaven,
      For His lovingkindness is everlasting." (vs. 26)

Part Three

THE SECOND ADVENT OF JESUS IN NEW TESTAMENT PROPHECY

"[We are to live] looking for the blessed hope and the appearing of the glory of our great God and Savior, Christ Jesus . . . — Titus 2:13

"He who testifies to these things says, 'Yes, I am coming quickly.' Amen. Come, Lord Jesus." —
Revelation 22:20

It's Almost Over

A song by Mike and Faye Speck ©

The winds of war keep raging through the land
    far and near,
The cry of hungry children, the pain, the falling
    tears.
Nations gather 'round the table, for peace
    they've tried for years;
Yet war still rages higher, sweeping through the
    battlefield.

We're living with the greatest promise that we
    will ever know;
The promise came from heaven of blessed peace
    and hope.
The battles, they keep raging higher, but we
    will have no fear;
The Savior's arms are open, and soon He shall
    appear.

It's almost over; we are going home.
Our Lord is coming to claim His own.
Be faithful children, brave and strong.
It's almost over; it's almost over;
It's almost over; we are going home!

A. INTRODUCTION

Moses prophesied that the Messiah would be a great prophet (Deuteronomy 18:15-18). The Gospels reveal that Jesus fulfilled this prophecy. He spoke prophetically many times concerning His future return to this earth.

The Gospels

The first sermon of Jesus' that you run across in the Gospels is His "Sermon on the Mount" recorded in Matthew 5-7. It begins with a remarkable series of prophetic statements:

> Blessed are the poor is spirit, for theirs
>   is the kingdom of heaven.
> Blessed are those who mourn, for they
>   shall be comforted.
> Blessed are the gentle, for they shall
>   inherit the earth. — Matthew 5:3-5

From that time to the end of His life, the sermons of Jesus were filled with prophetic references and statements. He was very conscious of fulfilling First Advent prophecies (see Luke 4:16-24). And He made frequent comments about His Second Advent. He stressed the certainty of His return and the fact that He would return in wrath to execute the vengeance of God.

Jesus also emphasized the certainty of judgment and reward for all — both the just and the unjust. He taught there would be degrees of blessing for the righteous and degrees of punishment for the unrighteous. He particularly focused on the rewards waiting for those who accepted Him in faith. He stressed the reward of eternal life, but He also outlined a breathtaking array of other rewards — some that would go to all believers and other, specialized awards, which would be given for distinguished service in the kingdom.

Jesus' most profound prophetic pronouncement was His "Olivet Discourse" delivered to His disciples on the Mount of Olives during the last week of His life. It provides a panoramic survey of the signs we are to look for which will signal the season of His return.

The Revelation of Jesus

The prophecies of Jesus do not end with the Gospels. Keep in mind that the book of Revelation is a revelation of Jesus to John. The letters to the seven churches of Asia, recorded in Revelation 2 and 3, are letters from Jesus. They contain many prophetic statements, particularly about the glorious rewards that await those who "overcome."

The New Testament ends with a prophetic pronouncement by Jesus. It contains His last recorded words: "Yes, I am coming quickly!" (Revelation 22:20).

The Epistles

Peter, Paul, and John often speak prophetically in the Epistles. Paul spends three full chapters in Romans (9-11) discussing the future salvation of a Jewish Remnant. In Romans 1:18-32 he gives us a detailed glimpse of the perverted nature of end time society. In Romans 8:18-25 he provides an inspiring picture of the future redemption of the universe.

Two of Paul's epistles, 1 and 2 Thessalonians, are almost entirely devoted to prophecy about the return of Christ. In these letters we find the most detailed description of the Rapture that is contained in the Bible (1 Thessalonians 4:13-18). Paul also gives a lot of detailed information about the "day of the Lord" in 1 Thessalonians 5 and 2 Thessalonians 2.

Most of what we know about the glorified bodies of the Redeemed comes from the description which Paul gives in 1 Corinthians 15 and 2 Corinthians 5. In his letters to Timothy, Paul elaborates on the signs that will signal the Lord's return, particularly the signs of society (2 Timothy 3:1-5). Paul also spends considerable time in his writings exhorting his readers to live godly lives as they look for the Second Coming (Romans 13, 1 Timothy 6, and Titus 2).

John's prophetic statements in his epistles relate almost exclusively to the antichrist spirit that will prevail in the end times (1 John 2:18-29). Peter writes much more extensively about the end times in his epistles. In 2 Peter 3 he prophesies the development of the scientific theory of Uniformitarianism, one of the cornerstones of Evolution. In that same passage, he provides a dramatic picture of the reshaping of the heavens and earth by fire.

The writer of Hebrews directs his prophetic comments toward the cosmic struggle for dominion over the earth. He points out that although Jesus won that dominion back from Satan by His work on the Cross, Jesus is not yet exercising that dominion, and will not do so until He returns to reign over the world (Hebrews 2:5-8).

The most ancient Second Coming prophecy in the Bible is contained in the book of Jude, verses 14-15. In these verses Jude quotes a vision attributed to Enoch in the seventh generation from Adam. In the vision Enoch saw the Lord returning to pour out the wrath of God on the ungodly.

The Revelation

The book of Revelation focuses on the Tribulation period and the wrath of God that will be poured out on all men to motivate them to repentance. It presents the story of the final crushing of Satan and the glorious triumph of Jesus. It provides a brief look at the Lord's millennial reign and then concludes with an intriguing glimpse of the incredible new Jerusalem that will serve as the eternal home of the Saints on the new earth.

One common myth that the following outline destroys is the idea that Revelation 20 provides all the information that the Bible contains about the Millennium. The truth is that Revelation 20 reveals very little information about the millennial reign. It tells us that the reign will last 1,000 years, but the Jewish Rabbis had deduced that long before Revelation was written. It says Satan will be bound at the beginning of the Millennium, something that can easily be deduced from Old Testament prophecies about the peace and righteousness that will prevail during that time. It states that the Saints will reign with Jesus, but that had already been specifically prophesied in many Old Testament passages (see, for example, Daniel 7:14, 18, 27). The revolt of Satan at the end of the Millennium is new information, but not the fact that his ultimate fate will be total defeat (Daniel 11:45).

If you will compare the previous outline of the Prophets (pages 56-65) with the following New Testament outline, you will easily see that the vast majority of the information we have about the nature of the Millennium is provided by Old Testament prophecy, particularly the prophecies of Isaiah. The Millennium is not a New Testament concept confined to one chapter in Revelation.

Revelation does provide us with our most detailed information about the Eternal State. Even so, what it reveals merely whets the appetite and stimulates the imagination. The fact of the matter is that the Bible tells us very little about the Eternal State except that the Redeemed will have glorified, immortal bodies and will live in God's presence in a new Jerusalem on a new earth. But what an exciting prospect that is! Romans 8:18 says "that the sufferings of this present time are not worthy to be compared with the glory that is to be revealed to us."

All I can say in response is, "Maranatha!" (1 Corinthians 16:22). ✤

B. AN OUTLINE OF SECOND ADVENT PROPHECIES IN THE NEW TESTAMENT

I. The Signs of the Times

A. Their Purpose — The signs will indicate the approaching return of the Lord.

". . . when you see all these things, recognize that He is near, right at the door." — Matthew 24:33 (Mark 13:29 and Luke 21:31).

B. Their Recognition — The Redeemed will be capable of recognizing the signs.

1) ". . . as you see the day drawing near." — Hebrews 10:25.

2) ". . . when these things begin to take place, straighten up and lift your heads, because your redemption is drawing near." — Luke 21:28.

3) "But you brethren, are not in darkness, that the day [of the Lord] should overtake you like a thief; for you are all sons of light and sons of day." — 1 Thessalonians 5:4-5.

C. The Nature of the Signs

They will be like "birth pangs;" that is, they will increase in frequency and intensity the closer we get to the Lord's return. — Matthew 24:6 and Mark 13:8.

D. The Kinds of Signs

1) Signs of Nature.

    a) Famines.
       Matthew 24:7; Mark 13:8; and Luke 21:11.

    b) Earthquakes.
       Matthew 24:7; Mark 13:8; and Luke 21:11.

    c) Pestilence (Plagues).
       Luke 21:11.

    d) Signs in the Heavens.
       Luke 21:11, 25.

2) Signs of Society.

    a) World society will be violent, sexually immoral, and caught up in the cares of the world.

(1) As in the days of Noah.
Matthew 24:37-38 and Luke 17:26-27.

(2) As in the days of Lot.
Luke 17:28-29.

b) Humanism will be the world's religion.

(1) People will worship the creature rather than the Creator.
Romans 1:22-23, 25.

(2) People will be "lovers of self."
2 Timothy 3:2.

(3) People will suppress the truth about God.
Romans 1:18-22, 30.

c) Materialism (money) will be the world's god.

(1) People will be "lovers of money."
2 Timothy 3:2.

(2) People will be greedy.
Romans 1:29 and 2 Timothy 3:2.

d) Hedonism will be the world's lifestyle.

(1) People will be "lovers of pleasure."
2 Timothy 3:4.

(2) People will give themselves over to sexual impurity.
Romans 1:24.

(3) There will be an outbreak of homosexuality.
Romans 1:26-27.

e) Nihilism (despair) will be the world's payoff for its ungodly attitudes and lifestyle.

(1) Alienation — "People's love will grow cold."
Matthew 24:12. See also Romans 1:28-32 and 2 Timothy 3:2-4.

(2) Lawlessness and Violence.
Matthew 24:12; Romans 1:29; and 2 Timothy 3:2-4.

(3) Arrogance and Boasting.
Romans 1:30 and 2 Timothy 3:2-4.

    (4) Deceit.
        Romans 1:29, 31 and 2 Timothy 3:2-4.

    (5) Maliciousness (gossip, slander, envy, and malice).
        Romans 1:29-30 and 2 Timothy 3:2-4.

    (6) Rebellious spirit among children.
        Romans 1:30 and 2 Timothy 3:2.

    (7) Betrayal by family members.
        Mark 13:12 and Luke 21:16.

    (8) Stress to the point that "men will faint from fear."
        Luke 21:26. See also 2 Timothy 3:1.

    (9) People to hate good.
        Romans 1:28-32 and 2 Timothy 3:3.

3) Spiritual Signs.

    a) Apostasy of the professing church.

        (1) Churches will present a form of religion that is devoid of power.
            2 Timothy 3:5.

        (2) There will be a "falling away from the faith" and some will betray one another. Matthew 24:10; 2 Thessalonians 2:3; 1 Timothy 4:1; and 2 Timothy 4:3-4.

        (3) People will reject sound doctrine and chase after myths.
            2 Timothy 4:1-4.

        (4) Certain ungodly persons will "turn the grace of our God into licentiousness." Jude 3-13.

        (5) There will be very little true faith on earth.
            Luke 18:8.

    b) Outbreak of false christs and false prophets.

        (1) False christs will mislead many.
            Matthew 24:5, 24; Mark 13:6, 21-22; and Luke 21:8.

        (2) False prophets will also mislead many.
            Matthew 24:11, 24 and Mark 13:22.

        (3) False christs and false prophets will perform "signs and wonders."
            Matthew 24:24 and Mark 13:22.

         (4)   Imposters will practice deception.
               2 Timothy 3:13.

         (5)   False teachers will introduce "destructive heresies."
               2 Peter 2:1-3.

         (6)   Deceptive religious leaders will operate in the spirit of the Antichrist.
               1 John 2:18-19.

    c)   Appearance of scoffers who will mock the idea of the Lord's return.
         Jude 17-18 and 2 Peter 3:3-4.

    d)   Persecution of believers.

         (1)   Believers will share the sufferings of Christ.
               Luke 21:12; 2 Timothy 3:12; and 1 Peter 4:12-14.

         (2)   Believers will be hated, persecuted and killed.
               Matthew 24:9; Mark 13:9; and Luke 21:17.

         (3)   Persecuted believers will be provided opportunities to witness Christ to Heads of State. Mark 13:9 and Luke 21:12-13.

    e)   Epidemic of occultic activity.
         1 Timothy 4:1.

    f)   The Gospel will be preached to all nations.
         Matthew 24:14 and Mark 13:10.

    g)   For other positive spiritual signs such as the understanding of prophecy, the revival of Davidic praise worship, and the pouring out of the Holy Spirit, see page 56 of the outline of Second Advent prophecies in the Old Testament.

4)   World Political Signs.

    a)   Nations will be distressed.
         Luke 21:25.

    b)   Class warfare will plague nations.
         James 5:1-6.

    c)   There will be wars and rumors of war.
         Matthew 24:6-7; Mark 13:7-8; and Luke 21:9-10.

    d)   There will be civil wars ("kingdom against kingdom").
         Matthew 24:7; Mark 13:8; and Luke 21:10.

    e)   A nation will exist in the East that is capable of sending an army of 200 million to Israel. Revelation 9:13-16 and Revelation 16:12.

f) A confederation of nations will be formed in the area of the old Roman Empire that will give rise to the Antichrist. Revelation 17:12-13.

g) The nation of Israel will exist again.
Matthew 24:32-34; Mark 13:28; and Luke 21:29-32.

5) Signs of Technology.

a) The "powers of the heavens will be shaken" (atomic power?).
Luke 21:26.

b) The return of Jesus is the only thing that will prevent Man from destroying all life (atomic weapons?). Matthew 24:22.

c) The scientific theory of Uniformitarianism will be developed (one of the cornerstones of Evolution). 2 Peter 3:4.

d) When the two witnesses of God are killed in the Tribulation, all the world will look upon their bodies for three days (television?). Revelation 11:8-9.

e) The False Prophet will make an image of the Antichrist that will appear to be alive (robotics?). Revelation 13:14-15.

f) The False Prophet will require everyone to wear the mark of the Antichrist in order to buy and sell (computers and lasers?). Revelation 13:17.

g) The Antichrist will control the entire world (rapid transportation and communication systems). Revelation 13:7.

6) The Signs of Israel.

a) The nation of Israel will exist again (May 14, 1948).
Matthew 24:32-34; Mark 13:28-30; and Luke 21:29-32.

b) The Jews will once again occupy and control the city of Jerusalem (June 7, 1967). Luke 21:24.

c) Many other signs of Israel in the end times are contained in Old Testament prophecies. See pages 56-57.

II. The Rapture

A. The Definition — The Lord will return to take the Redeemed out of the World.

1) "If I go and prepare a place for you, I will come again, and receive you to Myself, that where I am, there you may be also." — John 14:3.

2) ". . . with regard to the coming of our Lord Jesus Christ and our gathering together to Him . . ." 2 Thessalonians 2:1.

3) "I press on toward the prize of the upward call of God in Christ Jesus." — Philippians 3:14.

4) "For the Lord Himself will descend from heaven with a shout . . . and the dead in Christ shall rise first. Then we who are alive and remain shall be caught up [raptured] together with them in the clouds to meet the Lord in the air . . ." — 1 Thessalonians 4:16-17.

B. Distinction from the Second Advent — Instead of returning to the earth (as with the Second Coming), the Lord will appear or be revealed in the sky.

1) ". . . you are not lacking in any gift, awaiting eagerly the revelation of our Lord Jesus Christ . . ." — 1 Corinthians 1:7.

2) ". . . keep the commandment without stain or reproach until the appearing of our Lord Jesus Christ." — 1 Timothy 6:14.

3) "[We are to look] for the blessed hope and the appearing of the glory of our great God and Savior, Christ Jesus." — Titus 2:13.

4) ". . . fix your hope completely on the grace to be brought to you at the revelation of Jesus Christ." — 1 Peter 1:13.

5) "Then we who are alive and remain shall be caught up . . . to meet the Lord in the air . . ." — 1 Thessalonians 4:17.

C. Distinction from the Day of the Lord — As opposed to the "day of the Lord" when the Lord will return to the earth in wrath, the Rapture will be the "day of Christ" or the day of the Church's hope and redemption.

1) "For I am confident . . . that He who began a good work in you will perfect it until the day of Christ Jesus." — Philippians 1:6.

2) ". . . be sincere and blameless until the day of Christ . . ." — Philippians 1:10.

3) ". . . holding fast the word of life, so that in the day of Christ I may have cause to glory . . ." — Philippians 2:16.

4) "Do not grieve the Holy Spirit of God, by whom you were sealed for the day of redemption." — Ephesians 4:30.

5) "[We are to look] for the blessed hope and the appearing of the glory of our great God and Savior, Christ Jesus." — Titus 2:13.

6) "For we through the Spirit, by faith, are waiting for the hope of righteousness." — Galatians 5:5.

D. The Purpose of the Rapture — To deliver the Redeemed from the pouring out of God's wrath.

    1) "But keep on the alert at all times, praying in order that you may have strength to escape all these things that are about to take place, and stand before the Son of Man." — Luke 21:36.

    2) ". . . having now been justified by His blood, we shall be saved from the wrath of God through Him." — Romans 5:9.

    3) ". . . wait for His Son from heaven . . . who rescues us from the wrath to come." — 1 Thessalonians 1:10.

    4) "For God has not destined us to wrath, but for obtaining salvation through our Lord Jesus Christ." — 1 Thessalonians 5:9.

    5) ". . . Christ . . . will appear a second time for salvation without reference to sin, to those who eagerly await Him." — Hebrews 9:28.

E. The Timing of the Rapture — Before the Tribulation period of God's wrath.

    1) When the end time signs *begin* to take place, the Church is to look for its redemption. Luke 21:28.

    2) It will occur before the Day of the Lord.
    2 Thessalonians 2:1-2.

    3) It will occur before the Antichrist is revealed.
    2 Thessalonians 2:3-7.

    4) It will occur before the pouring out of God's wrath.
    1 Thessalonians 1:10, 1 Thessalonians 5:9 and Revelation 3:10.

    5) When Jesus returns at the Second Advent, the Saints come with Him — indicating that they must have ascended to heaven at an earlier time. Colossians 3:4; 1 Thessalonians 3:13; Revelation 17:14; and Revelation 19:14.

F. Prophetic Types of the Rapture — They provide confirmation of the event's pre-Tribulation timing.

    1) John's rapture to Heaven at the beginning of the Tribulation narrative in Revelation.
    Revelation 4:1-2.

    2) Noah and Lot were taken out before the execution of God's wrath — "The Lord knows how to rescue the godly from trial." — 2 Peter 2:4-9.

G. The Events of the Rapture

1) Jesus will descend from Heaven.
1 Thessalonians 4:16.

2) His descent will be signaled by a cry of command from Jesus, the shout of an archangel, and the blowing of the trumpet of God. John 5:25 and 1 Thessalonians 4:16.

3) These signals will be heard only by the Redeemed, living and dead.
John 5:25.

4) The Lord will be accompanied by the spirits of dead Saints.
1 Thessalonians 4:14.

5) The bodies of dead Saints will be resurrected (to be reunited with their spirits).
1 Thessalonians 4:15.

6) Then the living Saints will be caught up to meet the Lord in the air.
1 Thessalonians 4:15,17.

7) Both the resurrected Saints and those alive will then have their bodies glorified, making them immortal. 1 Corinthians 15:42-44, 51-53.

H. Sanctification and the Rapture — The Sanctification of the Redeemed will be completed with the Rapture.

1) "[Jesus Christ] will also confirm you to the end, blameless in the day of our Lord Jesus Christ." — 1 Corinthians 1:8.

2) ". . . that He might present to Himself the church in all her glory, having no spot or wrinkle or any such thing . . ." — Ephesians 5:27.

3) "For I am confident . . . that He who began a good work in you will perfect it until the day of Christ Jesus." — Philippians 1:6.

4) ". . . He has now reconciled you . . . in order to present you before Him holy and blameless and beyond reproach . . ." — Colossians 1:22.

5) "Now may the God of peace Himself sanctify you entirely . . . without blame at the coming of our Lord Jesus Christ." — 1 Thessalonians 5:23.

I. The Lord's Supper and the Rapture — The Lord's Supper is to serve as a reminder of the Lord's promise to come for His Church. 1 Corinthians 11:26.

III. The Resurrection of the Redeemed

A. The Certainty of the Resurrection

    1) Proved by God's continuing relationship with the Patriarchs after their deaths. Matthew 22:31-32; Mark 12:26-27; and Luke 20:37-38.

    2) Promised by Jesus. Luke 14:14; John 5:29; and John 14:1-4.

    3) Affirmed by Paul. Acts 24:15; Romans 6:5; 2 Corinthians 4:14; and Philippians 3:11.

B. Names of the Resurrection

    1) Resurrection of the "Just or "Righteous." Luke 14:14 and Acts 24:15.

    2) The "resurrection of life." John 5:29.

    3) The "resurrection from the dead." Philippians 3:11.

    4) The "first resurrection." Revelation 20:4-5.

C. The Resurrection to Occur in Stages — The stages will correspond to the three parts of a Jewish harvest: the first fruits, the general harvest, and the gleanings.

    1) Christ is the first fruits. 1 Corinthians 15:20.

    2) The general harvest — the resurrection of the Church (living and dead) will occur at the Rapture. 1 Corinthians 15:23.

    3) Old Testament Saints and Tribulation martyrs will constitute the gleanings to be resurrected at the Lord's Second Coming, at the end of the Tribulation. Revelation 20:4 (Daniel 12:1-2).

D. The Resurrection of the Church (the General Harvest)

    1) It will take place by the power of Jesus. John 6:39-40.

    2) It will be signaled by a cry of command from Jesus. John 5:25 and 1 Thessalonians 4:16.

3) It will occur at the blowing of the last trumpet.
1 Corinthians 15:52.

4) It will occur quickly, "in the twinkling of an eye."
1 Corinthians 15:52.

5) It will take place at the time of the Rapture.
1 Corinthians 15:22-23 and 1 Thessalonians 4:13-18.

IV. The Glorification of the Redeemed

A. The Time — Glorification occurs at the resurrection of the Righteous.

"For the anxious longing of the creation waits eagerly for the revealing of the sons of God [the resurrection of the just] . . . even we ourselves groan within ourselves, waiting eagerly for our adoption as sons, the redemption of our body." — Romans 8:19, 23. See also Philippians 1:6 and Philippians 3:21.

B. The Type of Body — The Redeemed receive immortality.

". . . they cannot even die anymore, because they are like angels, and are sons of God, being sons of the resurrection." — Luke 20:36.

C. The Nature of the Glorified Body

1) Imperishable.
1 Corinthians 15:42, 52-54.

2) Glorious.
1 Corinthians 15:43.

3) Powerful.
1 Corinthians 15:43.

4) Spiritual. (In the sense of being Spirit controlled.)
1 Corinthians 15:44.

5) Immortal, Eternal.
1 Corinthians 15:53-54 and 2 Corinthians 5:1.

6) Perfected — Numerous Old Testament passages indicate that the glorified body will be a perfected one. Thus, the blind will see, the lame will walk, the deaf will hear, the mute will speak, and the mentally disabled will have their minds healed. (See, for example, Isaiah 35:5-6.)

7) Like the resurrected, glorified body of Jesus.
Philippians 3:21.

a) Tangible.
Luke 24:39.

b) Identifiable.
John 21:1-7.

c) Capable of eating.
Luke 24:42-43 and John 21:10-15.

d) But with a different dimension.
Luke 24:36-37.

8) No marriage or procreation.
Matthew 22:30; Mark 12:25; and Luke 20:35.

V. The Judgment of the Redeemed

A. The Certainty of Judgment for All People — The Just and the Unjust

"For we shall all stand before the judgment seat of God . . . So then each of us will give an account of himself to God." — Romans 14:10, 12; 2 Corinthians 5:10; and John 5:25-29. See also Hebrews 9:27.

B. The Place and Time of the Judgment of the Redeemed

After the Rapture at the judgment seat of Christ.
2 Corinthians 5:10.

C. The Nature of the Judgment of the Righteous

1) *Not* for sin because that judgment took place at the Cross.
John 5:24; 2 Corinthians 5:21; Galatians 3:13; and Hebrews 9:28.

2) Rather, the Righteous will be judged of their works to determine their degrees of reward. Luke 19:11-27 and Romans 2:6-7.

a) The works of the Righteous will be judged as to their quantity.
2 Corinthians 5:10; Ephesians 2:10; Titus 2:14; Hebrews 13:15-16; James 1:26-27; and James 2:14, 20.

b) The works of the Righteous will be judged as to their quality.
Matthew 25:14-30 and 1 Corinthians 3:13.

c) The works of the Righteous will be judged as to their motives.
Matthew 19:27-30; 1 Corinthians 4:5; and 1 Corinthians 10:31.

D. The Degrees of Rewards — There will be degrees of rewards for the Righteous.

  1) The principle of degrees of reward.
Matthew 16:27; Romans 2:6-7; 1 Corinthians 3:13-15; 2 Corinthians 5:10; Colossians 3:23-24; Revelation 2:23; and Revelation 22:12.

  2) Examples of degrees of reward.

    a) Whatever a person gives up for the Lord he will receive back one hundred times over. Mark 10:29-30 and Luke 18:29-30.

    b) Those who are hated and persecuted for Christ will receive a great reward in Heaven. Matthew 5:11-12 and Luke 6:22-23.

    c) Those who show kindness to the poor, the maimed, the lame and the blind will be rewarded at the resurrection of the Righteous. Luke 14:12-14.

    d) Those who exalt themselves will be humbled and the humble will be exalted. Matthew 19:30; Mark 10:31; Luke 13:30; and Luke 14:11.

    e) Some will receive no reward other than eternal life. 1 Corinthians 3:13-15.

E. The Glorious Rewards of the Righteous

  1) Generalized Statements

    a) "For I consider that the sufferings of this present time are not worthy to be compared with the glory that is to be revealed to us." — Romans 8:18.

    b) ". . . no eye has seen, nor ear heard, nor the heart of man conceived, what God has prepared for those who love Him." — 1 Corinthians 2:9 (RSV).

    c) "For momentary, light affliction is producing for us an eternal weight of glory far beyond all comparison . . ." — 2 Corinthians 4:17.

    d) ". . . in order that in the ages to come He might show the surpassing riches of His grace in kindness toward us in Christ Jesus." — Ephesians 2:7.

  2) Rewards Given at the Appearing of Christ (The Rapture)

    a) The Rapture — ". . . the prize of the upward call of God in Christ Jesus." Philippians 3:14.

    b) Deliverance from death. John 11:25-26.

c) Power over the "second death."
Revelation 2:11 and Revelation 20:6.

d) Bodies glorified like the body of Christ.
Romans 8:23, 30; 1 Corinthians 15:35-53; and Philippians 3:21.

e) Souls conformed to the image of Christ.
Romans 8:29-30; 1 Peter 1:4-5, 9; and 1 John 3:2.

f) Eternal life.
Matthew 19:29; Matthew 25:46; Mark 10:30; Luke 18:30; John 3:15-16; John 5:24; John 6:27, 40, 47, 51-54; John 11:25-26; John 12:25, 50; John 17:3; Acts 13:46, 48; Romans 2:7; Romans 5:21; Romans 6:22-23; Galatians 6:8; Titus 1:2; Titus 3:7; Hebrews 9:281 Peter 1:4; 1 John 2:17, 25; 1 John 5:11, 13; Jude 21; Revelation 2:7; Revelation 2:11; Revelation 3:5; Revelation 3:12; and Revelation 21:1-7

3) Rewards Given at the Throne of God in Heaven.

a) Be presented to God by Christ without blemish and with rejoicing.
Jude 24.

b) Be confessed by Christ before the Father and His angels.
Matthew 10:32; Luke 12:8; and Revelation 3:5.

c) See God.
Matthew 5:8.

d) Be honored by the Father by being perfected, confirmed, strengthened and established. John 12:26 and 1 Peter 5:10.

e) Be adopted as the sons of God.
Romans 8:23.

4) Rewards Given at the Judgment Seat of Christ in Heaven.

a) Name included in the book of life.
Revelation 3:5.

b) No judgment for sin.
John 5:24 and Hebrews 9:28

c) Sins forgiven and forgotten.
Hebrews 8:12 and Hebrews 10:17.

d) Receive a white stone, signifying innocence.
Revelation 2:17.

e) Remembrance of good deeds by God.
Hebrews 6:10.

f) Receive a new name.
Revelation 2:17.

g) Receive God's rest from troubles, toils and afflictions.
Matthew 11:28-30; 2 Thessalonians 1:7; and Hebrews 4:3-10.

h) Full understanding of all God's mysteries.
1 Corinthians 13:12.

i) Be made a pillar in the temple of God.
Revelation 3:12.

j) Receive some of the hidden manna.
Revelation 2:17.

k) Be acknowledged as belonging to God the Father,
His city, and His Son. Revelation 3:12.

5) Specialized Rewards Given at the Judgment Seat of Christ.

a) Comfort for those who mourned.
Matthew 5:4 and Luke 6:21.

b) Satisfaction for those who hungered and thirsted for righteousness.
Matthew 5:6 and Luke 6:21.

c) Mercy for those who were merciful.
Matthew 5:7.

d) A great reward of praise, honor and glory for those who were persecuted.
Matthew 5:10-12; Luke 6:22-23; and 1 Peter 1:7.

e) For those who were sacrificial, they will receive back a hundred times more
than what they surrendered for Christ. Matthew 19:29.

f) Exaltation for those who were humble.
Matthew 18:4.

g) Special blessings for those who rendered special services to the Church.
2 Timothy 1:16-18.

h) An imperishable wreath for those who exercised self-control.
1 Corinthians 9:24-27.

i) A crown of exaltation for those who were soul winners.
1 Thessalonians 2:19-20.

j) A crown of righteousness for those who loved the Lord's appearing.
2 Timothy 4:8.

k) A crown of life for those who endured trials.
James 1:12.

l) An unfading crown of glory for those who served as elders.
1 Peter 5:1-4.

6) Rewards Given at the End of the Tribulation Period

a) Invitation to attend the marriage feast of the Lamb.
Revelation 19:9.

b) Special robes of fine linen, clean and bright.
Revelation 3:5 and Revelation 19:8.

c) Celebration of a great feast with Jesus.
Matthew 22:1-10; Luke 14:15-24; and Revelation 19:7-9.

d) The Lord's Supper is to serve as a reminder of the Lord's promise to celebrate a great feast with His Church. Matthew 26:29; Mark 14:25; and Luke 22:18.

7) Rewards Given at the Return of Christ to the Earth (the Second Advent).

a) Inherit the earth.
Matthew 5:5 and Romans 4:13.

b) Inherit the kingdom.
Matthew 5:3 and James 2:5.

c) Reign with Jesus over the world.
2 Timothy 2:12; Revelation 2:26-27; Revelation 3:21; and Revelation 5:10.

d) Exercise various degrees of ruling power.
Luke 19:11-27.

e) Be glorified with Jesus.
Matthew 13:43; Romans 2:10; Romans 8:17; and 2 Thessalonians 1:10.

VI. The Tribulation

A. The Concept — A World-Wide Period of Judgment

    1) ". . . there will be a great tribulation, such has not occurred since the beginning of the world until now, nor ever will." — Matthew 24:21.

    2) ". . . the Lord knows how . . . to keep the unrighteous under punishment for the day of judgment . . ." — 2 Peter 2:9.

    3) ". . . the hour of testing, that hour which is about to come upon the whole world, to test those who dwell upon the earth." — Revelation 3:10.

B. The Nature of the Tribulation

    1) Days of God's vengeance.
       Luke 21:22.

    2) A time for the pouring out of God's wrath.
       Romans 5:9; 1 Thessalonians 1:10; and Revelation 15:1.

    3) A period of unparalleled strife.
       Matthew 24:21 and Mark 13:19.

    4) The conflict will be so great that the return of Christ will be the only thing that will prevent humanity from destroying itself. Matthew 24:22 and Mark 13:20.

C. The Length of the Tribulation — Seven Years

    1) Two witnesses of God will prophesy for 1,260 days (3½ years by the Jewish calendar of 360 days in a year) before being killed by the Antichrist. Revelation 11:3, 7.

    2) The Antichrist will then be given authority to act for 42 months (another 3½ years). Revelation 13:5.

D. The Key Events of the Tribulation

    1) God pours out His wrath in the Seal Judgments. One-fourth of humanity dies from war, famine, pestilence and wild beasts. Revelation 6:1-8.

    2) 144,000 Jews are sealed by God and are sent forth as His servants.
       Revelation 7:1-8.

    3) Two special witnesses of God are commissioned to prophesy to the world.
       Revelation 11:3-6.

    4) There is an indication that those who heard the Gospel before the Rapture and rejected it are deceived during the Tribulation and continue to reject the Gospel. 2 Thessalonians 2:11-12.

5) The vast majority of humanity refuses to repent. Revelation 9:20-21.

6) But the missionary Jews and the two special witnesses still produce a great harvest of souls for the Lord, most of whom suffer martyrdom. Revelation 7:9-17.

7) God pours out His second series of judgments — the Trumpet Judgments. One-third of those left alive die from fire and pollution of the world's water supplies. Revelation 8 and 9.

8) A war breaks out in Heaven as Satan tries one last time to take the throne of God. Revelation 12:7-8.

9) Satan is defeated and cast down to the earth in great wrath. Revelation 12:9-12.

10) Satan empowers the Antichrist who arises out of a resurrected Roman Empire. 2 Thessalonians 2:9; Revelation 13:1-3; and Revelation 17:9-14.

11) The Antichrist blasphemes God and defiles the rebuilt Temple by entering the Holy Place and declaring himself to be God. Matthew 24:15; Mark 13:14; 2 Thessalonians 2:3-4; 1 John 2:22; and Revelation 13:5-6.

12) The Antichrist kills the two witnesses of God. Revelation 11:7-8.

13) The Antichrist begins a great persecution of all Jews and Christians. Revelation 13:5-7.

14) The Jewish Remnant flees to the wilderness where they are supernaturally protected and nourished by God. Matthew 24:15-21; Mark 13:14-18; and Revelation 12:6, 13-17.

15) The Antichrist is received by the world and establishes a world-wide government. John 5:43 and Revelation 13:7-8.

16) An apostate world church becomes a rival to the Antichrist, and he destroys it. Revelation 17.

17) The Antichrist is assisted by a False Prophet who leads the world in worship of the Antichrist. Revelation 13:3-4, 8, 11-15.

18) No one is allowed to buy or sell without having the mark of the Antichrist. Revelation 13:16-18.

19) The Antichrist's kingdom, called "Babylon the great," accumulates enormous wealth. Revelation 18.

20) The Antichrist is engaged in constant wars as he tries to hold his world empire together. The focus of activity is Jerusalem, and the city is trampled for 3½ years. Revelation 11:1-2.

21) God sends forth an angel to proclaim the Gospel to all the world and to call for repentance. Revelation 14:6-7.

22) God sends forth a second angel to prophesy to all the world the fall of the Antichrist's kingdom. Revelation 14:8.

23) God sends forth a third angel to warn all the world against taking the mark of the Antichrist. Revelation 14:9-11.

24) God pours out His wrath in a final series of Bowl Judgments, afflicting humanity with sores, heat, darkness and pollution of all water. Revelation 16.

25) The greatest earthquake in all of history occurs, radically changing the earth's topography. Revelation 6:12-17 and Revelation 16:17-21.

26) The kingdom of the Antichrist is destroyed. Revelation 18.

27) The Saints in Heaven rejoice over the judgments of God and celebrate the Marriage Feast of the Lamb. Revelation 19:1-10.

28) Jesus bursts from the heavens with His bride, the Church, to return to earth as King of kings. Revelation 19:11-16.

29) The Battle of Armageddon results in the triumph of Jesus over the Antichrist and the False Prophet and their forces. 2 Thessalonians 2:8; Revelation 16:16; Revelation 17:14; and Revelation 19:17-21.

30) The Antichrist and False Prophet are thrown into the lake of fire (Hell) where they are tormented forever. Revelation 19:20 and Revelation 20:10.

VII. The Second Coming of Jesus

A. The Timing of the Lord's Return

1) The Return will occur on a date that has been fixed by God. Acts 17:31.

2) The Return will be signaled by signs which Believers can recognize. Matthew 24:33; Mark 13:29; and Luke 21:31.

3) The Return of the Lord will occur at a time when the fig tree blossoms — that is, when Israel exists again as a nation. Matthew 24:32-35; Mark 13:28-31; and Luke 21:29-32. (Fulfilled May 14, 1948.)

4) The people who witness the re-establishment of Israel are the ones who will see all the end time events come to pass. Matthew 24:34; Mark 13:30; and Luke 21:32.

5) The Return of the Lord will occur at a time when the Jews are once again in control of Jerusalem. Luke 21:24. (Fulfilled June 7, 1967.)

6) The Return will occur at a time when the full number of the Gentiles have been brought into the Church. Romans 11:25-26.

7) The Return will occur at a time when there is little faith left in the world. Luke 18:8.

8) The Return will be preceded by the preaching of Elijah (one of the two witnesses of the first half of the Tribulation?). Matthew 17:11.

9) The Return will occur after the revelation of the Antichrist. 2 Thessalonians 2:2-3.

10) The Return will occur at the end of the Tribulation. Matthew 24:29 and Mark 13:24.

11) The Return will be preceded by the repentance of the Jewish Remnant. Matthew 23:39 and Luke 13:35.

12) The Return will occur suddenly, like lightening. Matthew 24:27 and Luke 17:24. See also Mark 13:33-37.

13) The Return will occur at a time when the world least expects it — like "a thief in the night." Matthew 24:42-43; Mark 13:33-37; Luke 12:35-40; 1 Thessalonians 5:2-5; 2 Peter 3:10; Revelation 3:3; and Revelation 16:15.

   a) The parable of the just and unjust servants. Matthew 24:45-51 and Luke 12:42-46.

   b) The parable of the ten virgins. Matthew 25:1-13.

   c) The parable of the watchful servant. Mark 13:32-37.

14) No one can know the exact day or hour of the Return. Matthew 24:36, 42, 44 and Mark 13:32.

15) The Return will occur soon.

   a) "The end of all things is near . . ." — 1 Peter 4:7 and James 5:8.

   b) ". . . it is the last hour . . ." — 1 John 2:18.

    c) "Yet in a very little while, He who is coming will come, and will not delay." — Hebrews 10:37 (quote of Habakkuk 2:3). See James 5:7-8.

    d) ". . . things which must soon take place . . . for time is near." — Revelation 1:1, 3. See also Revelation 22:10.

    e) "And behold, I am coming quickly." — Revelation 22:7; 12, 20.

    f) "But do not let this one fact escape your notice, beloved, that with the Lord one day is as a thousand years . . . The Lord is not slow about His promise, as some count slowness, but is patient toward you, not wishing for any to perish but for all to come to repentance." — 2 Peter 3:8-9.

B. The Nature of the Day When the Lord Returns

    1) A day of darkness.
        Matthew 24:29; Mark 13:24; Acts 2:20; and Revelation 6:12.

    2) A day of vengeance.
        Luke 21:22.

    3) A day of God's wrath.
        Romans 2:5 and 1 Thessalonians 1:10.

    4) A day of mourning.
        Matthew 24:30 and Revelation 1:7.

C. The Nature of the Lord's Return

    1) The Return will be signaled by the blast of a great trumpet.
        Matthew 24:31.

    2) The Lord will come in the clouds of heaven.
        Matthew 24:30; Matthew 26:64; Mark 13:26; Mark 14:62; Luke 21:27; and Revelation 1:7.

    3) Jesus will break from the heavens riding a white horse.
        Revelation 19:11.

    4) The Return will be visible to all humanity.
        Matthew 24:30; Mark 13:26; and Revelation 1:7.

    5) The Lord will return in wrath.
        Revelation 6:15-17

        a) As a mighty warrior with a robe dipped in blood.
            Revelation 19:13.

        b) Revealed in flaming fire.
            2 Thessalonians 1:7.

        c) Political leaders will hide and cry for death.
            Revelation 6:15-16.

   6) The Lord will return in power.
      Matthew 24:30; Mark 13:26; and Luke 21:27.

   7) The Lord will return in righteousness.
      Revelation 19:11.

   8) The Lord will return in great glory.
      Matthew 16:27; Matthew 24:30; Matthew 25:31; Mark 8:38; Mark 13:26; Luke 9:26; Luke 21:27; and Colossians 3:4.

   9) The Lord will return with His angels.
      Matthew 16:27; Mark 8:38; Luke 9:26; and 2 Thessalonians 1:7.

  10) The Lord will return with His Saints.
      Colossians 3:4; 1 Thessalonians 3:13; Revelation 17:14; and Revelation 19:14.

D. Natural Phenomena Associated with the Lord's Return

   1) There will be signs in the heavens — sun and moon darkened, stars falling, powers shaken and the sky rolled up. Matthew 24:29-30; Mark 13:24-25; Acts 2:19-20; and Revelation 6:12-14.

   2) The earth will be completely reshaped by the greatest earthquake in history. Revelation 6:12, 14 and Revelation 16:18-20.

E. The Purposes of the Lord's Return

   1) To make war against the enemies of God.
      Revelation 19:11.

   2) To execute God's vengeance.
      Romans 12:19; 2 Thessalonians 1:7-8; Hebrews 10:30-31; Jude 14-15; Revelation 6:9-11; and Revelation 19:2. See the parable of the wicked tenants in Matthew 21:33-46; Mark 12:1-12; and Luke 20:9-18.

   3) To pour out God's wrath.
      John 3:36; Romans 2:5; Romans 5:9; Colossians 3:6; 1 Thessalonians 1:10; Revelation 6:16-17; Revelation 11:18; Revelation 14:19-20; and Revelation 19:15.

   4) To execute God's judgment.
      John 5:27; Acts 10:42; Acts 17:31; Romans 2:5; 1 Corinthians 4:5; 2 Timothy 4:1; Hebrews 10:30; James 5:9; Jude 14-15; Revelation 11:18; Revelation 14:14-20; and Revelation 19:11.

5) To take dominion over the earth.
Revelation 5:9-10, 13 and Revelation 10:1-7.

6) To reign as King of kings.
1 Timothy 6:15; Revelation 17:14; and Revelation 19:12, 16.

7) To manifest His glory.
2 Thessalonians 1:10; 1 Peter 4:13; and Revelation 5:12.

Note: The Transfiguration was a preview of the glory which Jesus will manifest at His return. Matthew 17:1-8; Mark 9:2-8; and Luke 9:28-35.

F. The Gatherings Which Will Occur at the Lord's Return

1) The gathering of the Unjust.
Revelation 14:17-20.

a) Unjust to be gathered first — before the Just.
Matthew 13:30, 41-42, 49-50.

b) The effect will be like the Rapture — one taken, one left behind.
Matthew 24:40-41 and Luke 17:34-37.

2) The gathering of the Just (those who accept Christ during the Tribulation and live to the end). Matthew 3:12; Matthew 13:30; Matthew 24:31; Mark 13:27; and Revelation 14:14-16.

G. The Resurrections Which Will Occur at the Lord's Return

1) Old Testament Saints who lived and died before the Church Age (Church Age Saints are resurrected at the Rapture). The timing of this resurrection is established by Daniel 12:1-2. It is implied in the New Testament in Matthew 19:28-30.

2) The Tribulation Saints who were martyred by the Antichrist.
Revelation 20:4.

H. The Judgments Which Will Occur at the Lord's Return

1) Jesus will judge the Gentiles — both the Just and the Unjust.
Matthew 25:31-46.

a) The Unjust will be slain before the Lord, fed to vultures and consigned to Hell.
Matthew 25:41; Luke 17:34-37; and Luke 19:27.

b) The Just will be allowed to enter the millennial kingdom in the flesh and will be destined for eternal life. Matthew 25:34, 46.

c) The glorified Saints of the Church Age will assist Jesus with these judgments.
1 Corinthians 6:2.

2) Jesus will judge the resurrected Tribulation martyrs.
Implied by Revelation 20:4.

3) The Apostles will judge the Jews (both the Jewish Remnant alive in the flesh at the end of the Tribulation and the glorified Jews resurrected at the end of the Tribulation). Matthew 19:28 and Luke 22:28-30.

4) The glorified Saints of the Church will judge the angels.
1 Corinthians 6:3 and Jude 6.

VIII. The Millennium

A. The Purposes of the Millennium

1) To fulfill prophecy.
Luke 24:44 and Acts 3:20-21.

2) To fulfill God's promise that Jesus will manifest His glory in a world-wide reign.
Luke 1:32-33; 2 Thessalonians 1:10; and Revelation 5:9-13.

3) To fulfill God's promise that the Saints will be blessed by ruling with Jesus over the world. 2 Timothy 2:12; Revelation 2:26-27; Revelation 3:21; Revelation 5:9-10; and Revelation 20:4.

4) To fulfill God's earthly promises to the Jews (specifically to a believing Remnant). Romans 3:1-4; Romans 4:13; Romans 9:1-5, 27; and Romans 11:1-6, 25-32.

5) To fulfill God's promise to restore His creation.
Acts 3:19-21 and Romans 8:18-23.

6) To prove that evil is rooted within Man and not society (for after 1,000 years of peace, righteousness and justice, Man will still revolt against God). Mark 7:20-22 and Revelation 20:7-10.

7) To consummate the destruction of all the enemies of Jesus.

a) Satan to be crushed.
Romans 16:20 and Revelation 20:10.

b) Death to be destroyed.
1 Corinthians 15:26, 54-57.

c) All enemies of God to be put under the feet of Jesus.
1 Corinthians 15:24-25; Hebrews 2:5-8; and Hebrews 10:12-13.

B. The Nature of the Millennial Kingdom

1) Jesus will reign over the whole world from the throne of David.
Matthew 19:28; Luke 1:32-33; Revelation 3:21; Revelation 11:15; Revelation 12:5, and Revelation 20:4.

2) The Lord's reign will last for 1,000 years. Revelation 20:4-7.

3) The redeemed and glorified Saints (Old Testament, Church Age and Tribulation Saints) will reign with Jesus. 2 Timothy 2:12; Revelation 2:26-27; Revelation 3:21, Revelation 5:10; and Revelation 20:4, 6.

4) The Lord's kingdom will not be "of" this world (that is, it will not be a kingdom based upon political relationships and political power). John 18:36.

5) The kingdom will be a theocracy in which Jesus will serve as both King and Priest.

   a) "King of kings."
      1 Timothy 6:15; Revelation 17:14; and Revelation 19:12, 16.

   b) "Chief Shepherd."
      1 Peter 5:4.

6) Jesus will rule absolutely "with a rod of iron" as "Lord of lords."

   a) "Rod of iron."
      Revelation 2:27; Revelation 12:5; and Revelation 19:15.

   b) "Lord of lords."
      1 Timothy 6:15; Revelation 17:14; and Revelation 19:16.

C. Characteristics of the Millennial Kingdom

1) The will of the Father will be done on earth as it is in Heaven. Matthew 6:10.

2) There will be an atmosphere of peace and joy and righteousness as all the nations worship God. Romans 14:17 and Revelation 15:4.

3) There will be intimate fellowship with the Lord. Matthew 8:11; Luke 13:29; Luke 14:15-24; Luke 22:30; and Revelation 3:20.

4) It will be a kingdom of humble service. Matthew 18:1-5; Matthew 20:20-28; Mark 9:33-37; Mark 10:35-45; Luke 1:51-52; Luke 9:46-48; and Luke 22:24-29.

D. Satan's Activity during the Millennium

1) Satan will be bound at the beginning of the Lord's millennial reign so that he can no longer deceive the nations. Revelation 20:1-3.

2) Satan will be let loose at the end of the Millennium to deceive the nations, exposing the rebellion that has been lurking in Men's hearts. Revelation 20:7-8.

3) Satan will lead a world wide revolt against the reign of Jesus, proving that Men's hearts cannot be changed by the perfection of society. Revelation 20:8-9.

4) Satan's revolt will be ended by fire from Heaven. Revelation 20:9.

5) Satan will be thrown into the lake of fire where he will be tormented forever, together with the Antichrist and False Prophet. Revelation 20:10.

IX. The Judgment of the Unjust

A. The Resurrection of the Unjust
Acts 24:15.

1) It will be the "second resurrection." (The "first resurrection" — the resurrection of the just — occurs in three stages. See III-C on page 103) Revelation 20:4-5.

2) It will be a "resurrection of judgment" (as opposed to a "resurrection of life"). John 5:29.

3) It will occur at the end of the Millennium. Revelation 20:11-15.

B. The Great White Throne Judgment. Revelation 20:11-15.

1) This judgment is certain to occur. Romans 14:10, 12 and Hebrews 9:27.

2) The wrath of God will rest upon those to be judged. John 3:36.

3) It is a judgment of the damned because they will be judged by their works, and no Man can be justified by his works. Romans 2:5-8; Romans 3:28; Ephesians 2:8-9; and Revelation 20:12.

4) Some of those condemned will have done works in the name of Jesus. Matthew 7:21-23.

5) Each person will have to account for every careless word spoken. Matthew 12:36.

6) Jesus will expose and judge the secrets of each person's heart. Romans 2:16.

7) Those who denied Jesus will be denied by Him before the Father and His angels. Matthew 10:33; Luke 12:9; and 2 Timothy 2:12.

8) Those who were ashamed of Jesus will experience shame before Him. Mark 8:38 and Luke 9:26.

9) There will be no forgiveness for those who have blasphemed the Spirit (that is, those who rejected the Spirit's witness of Jesus). Matthew 12:32.

10) Every knee shall bow and every tongue confess that Jesus is Lord. Romans 14:11 and Philippians 2:10-11.

11) The Unjust will not inherit the kingdom of God. 1 Corinthians 6:9-10 and Galatians 5:19-21.

C. The Destiny of the Unjust

   1) The Unjust will not receive eternal life. John 3:36.

   2) The Unjust will be excluded from the presence of God. 2 Thessalonians 1:9.

   3) The Unjust will receive an eternal punishment. Matthew 25:46.

   4) The Unjust will taste the wrath and fury of God in distress and affliction. Romans 2:8-9; Ephesians 5:6; and 2 Thessalonians 1:6.

   5) The Unjust will be put in a place where there is weeping and gnashing of teeth. Matthew 8:12; Matthew 13:50; Matthew 22:13; Matthew 24:51; Matthew 25:30; and Luke 13:28.

      a) "the outer darkness." — Matthew 8:12 and Matthew 22:13.

      b) "the furnace of fire." — Matthew 13:49-50.

      c) "a place with the hypocrites." — Matthew 24:51.

   6) The abode of the Unjust will be Hell (Gehenna). Mark 9:43-48 and Luke 12:5.

      a) A place prepared for the Devil and his angels. Matthew 25:41.

      b) A place where the Devil, the Antichrist and the False Prophet will be tormented forever. Revelation 19:20 and Revelation 20:10.

      c) A "furnace of fire." — Matthew 13:42.

      d) A "lake of fire." — Revelation 20:14-15 and Revelation 21:8.

e) A place of eternal fire.
   Matthew 3:12; Matthew 25:41; and Mark 9:43, 48.

f) A place of torment with fire and brimstone.
   Revelation 14:10-11.

7) The Unjust will experience degrees of punishment in Hell, proportional to their sins. Matthew 10:14-15; Matthew 11:20-24; Matthew 12:42; Luke 10:10-15; Luke 12: 47-48; Luke 20:45-47; and Colossians 3:25.

8) The ultimate destiny of the Unjust.

a) The Unjust will perish.
   Luke 13:3, 5 and John 3:16.

b) The Unjust will be destroyed — both body and soul.
   Matthew 10:28; Philippians 3:17-19; 2 Thessalonians 1:9; and 2 Peter 3:7.

c) The Unjust will be burned up.
   Matthew 13:30.

d) The Unjust will experience a "wretched end."
   Matthew 21:41.

e) The Unjust will experience the "second death."
   Revelation 20:14.

X. Eternity

A. The Eternal Kingdom

1) At the end of the Millennium, the Theocratic Kingdom of Jesus on earth will be merged with the Universal Kingdom of God in Heaven. 1 Corinthians 15:24-28.

2) Jesus will inherit all of God's creation.
   Hebrews 1:2.

3) All of creation will be put in subjection under Jesus.
   Hebrews 2:7-10.

4) Jesus will reign eternally.
   Luke 1:32-33; 1 Timothy 1:17; Hebrews 1:8; 1 Peter 4:11; 1 Peter 5:11; 2 Peter 1:11; Jude 25; and Revelation 11:15.

5) The Saints will reign eternally with Jesus.
   Revelation 22:5.

B. The New Heavens and Earth

1) God will make all things new.
Revelation 21:5.

2) The present heavens and earth will "pass away" as they are renovated with fire, producing the new heavens and earth. Matthew 5:18; Matthew 24:35; Mark 13:31; Luke 21:33; Hebrews 1:10-12; Hebrews 12:26-27; 2 Peter 3:10-13; and Revelation 21:1.

3) The new Jerusalem will descend from Heaven to rest on the new earth.
Revelation 21:2, 10.

4) The eternal abode of the redeemed Saints will be the new Jerusalem on the new earth. Revelation 21:1-7, 27 and Revelation 22:14.

5) God will come down from Heaven to live in the midst of His people on the new earth. Revelation 21:3, 22-23.

6) Nations* will exist on the new earth, but they will live outside the new Jerusalem. Revelation 21:24-27 and Revelation 22:2.

*Note: One of the great mysteries of prophecy is the identity of these nations. They are composed of people who sin (Revelation 21:27) and who need healing (Revelation 22:2). They are evidently the people who will be the subjects of the eternal reign of Jesus and His Saints. But it is never made plain who they are or where they come from. Perhaps they are the people who are alive at the end of the Millennium who have accepted Jesus as Lord and Savior.

C. The New Jerusalem

1) Designed and built by God.
Hebrews 11:10, 16 and Hebrews 12:22.

2) Enlarged by Jesus to provide room for His Bride, the Church.
John 14:1-4.

3) The Old Testament Saints longed for it.
Hebrews 11:8-10, 13-16.

4) The New Testament Saints longed for it.
Hebrews 13:14.

5) The city descends from Heaven to the new earth.
Revelation 21:2, 10.

6) The city is incredibly beautiful.

   a) Like a bride adorned for her husband.
      Revelation 21:2, 9.

   b) It has the glory of God.
      Revelation 21:11.

   c) It has a radiance like a rare jewel.
      Revelation 21:11.

   d) It has walls of jasper.
      Revelation 21:18.

   e) Its foundation is adorned with jewels.
      Revelation 21:19-20.

   f) Its gates are pearls.
      Revelation 21:21.

   g) Its buildings and streets are made of gold.
      Revelation 21:18, 21.

7) The city's construction details.

   a) The city is a cube 1,500 miles in length, width, and height.
      Revelation 21:16.

   b) Its foundation is composed of 12 layers of stone adorned with jewels, each
      layer containing the name of an Apostle. Revelation 21:14, 19-20.

   c) It is surrounded by a jasper wall 216 feet high.
      Revelation 21:12, 17-18.

   d) The wall has 12 pearl gates with a name of a tribe of Israel inscribed on each
      gate. Revelation 21:12.

   e) The buildings and streets are made of gold as clear as glass.
      Revelation 21:18, 21.

8) Other features of the city.

   a) There will be no night there.
      Revelation 21:25 and Revelation 22:5.

   b) The city will not need sun or moon, for the glory of God will illuminate it, and
      the Lamb will be its lamp. Revelation 21:23 and Revelation 22:5.

c) There will be no temple in the city "for the Lord God the Almighty and the Lamb are its temple." Revelation 21:22.

d) The city will contain the throne of God and the Lamb. Revelation 22:1.

e) Nothing unclean or evil will be allowed to enter the city. Revelation 21:27 and Revelation 22:15.

f) The kings of the nations outside the city will be allowed to bring their glory into it. Revelation 21:24.

g) A "river of the water of life" will flow from God's throne down the middle of the main street of the city. Revelation 22:1-2.

h) The tree of life will grow on both sides of the river and will bear twelve kinds of fruit, one for each month. Revelation 22:2.

i) The leaves of the tree of life will be used for the healing of the nations outside the city. Revelation 22:2.

D. The Blessings of the Redeemed in the Eternal State

1) The presence of God the Father and Jesus the Lamb. Revelation 21:3, 22-23 and Revelation 22:3-4.

2) Personal fellowship with God the Father and Jesus the Lamb. Revelation 21:3, 7 and Revelation 22:4.

3) Residence in the new Jerusalem. Revelation 3:12 and Revelation 22:14.

4) Access to the water of life. Revelation 7:17 and Revelation 21:6.

5) Access to the tree of life. Revelation 22:14.

6) Death will be abolished. Revelation 21:4.

7) There will be no pain or sorrow or mourning. Revelation 7:17 and Revelation 21:4.

8) There will be no more hunger or thirst. Revelation 7:16.

9) There will no longer be any curse — and thus there will be no deterioration of anything. Matthew 6:20 and Revelation 22:3.

10) The Redeemed will belong to God.
Revelation 21:7 and Revelation 22:4.

11) The Redeemed will worship and serve God.
Revelation 22:3.

12) Righteousness will characterize everything.
2 Peter 3:13.

13) The Redeemed will reign eternally with Jesus.
Revelation 22:5.

"And He who sits on the throne said, 'Behold, I am making all things new.' . . . Then He said to me, 'It is done, I am the Alpha and the Omega, the beginning and the end . . . He who overcomes shall inherit these things, and I will be his God and he will be My son.'"
— Revelation 21:5-7.

Stamped on the Universe

C. EPILOGUE

There are many things that we as Christians are exhorted and commanded to do as we serve the Lord. But the New Testament makes it very clear that there are some things we are to do in particular as we look for the return of Jesus.

Christian conduct for the end times is summarized in outline form below. The scripture references are taken only from passages that clearly have an end time context.

These passages make it clear that holy living is connected to an awareness that the Lord may return at any moment. So also is evangelism.

The greater the awareness a person has of the Lord's imminent return, the greater will be that person's motivation to live a holy life and to share the Gospel with others. ✤

Christian Conduct As We Await the Lord's Return

"Beloved, now we are children of God, and it has not appeared as yet what we will be. We know that when He appears, we will be like Him, because we will see Him just as He is. *And everyone who has this hope fixed on Him purifies himself*, just as He is pure." — 1 John 3:2-3 (Emphasis added.)

A. **Personal Conduct**

1) Holiness

   a) Be holy.
      1 Peter 1:13-16 and 2 Peter 3:11.

   b) Behave properly.
      Romans 13:13.

   c) Lead a life worthy of God.
      1 Thessalonians 2:12.

   d) Abide in Jesus.
      1 John 2:28.

   e) Aim at godliness.
      1 Timothy 6:11; Titus 2:12; 2 Peter 1:6; 2 Peter 3:11.

   f) Exercise moral excellence.
      2 Peter 1:5.

   g) Live sensibly.
      Titus 2:12.

2) Perseverance

    a) Be patient.
       James 5:7.

    b) Endure suffering.
       2 Thessalonians 1:4; 1 Timothy 6:11; Hebrews 10:36; 1 Peter 1:6-7; 2 Peter 1:6; and
       Revelation 14:12.

3) Faith

    a) Pursue faith.
       1 Timothy 6:11 and 2 Peter 1:5.

    b) Live by faith.
       Hebrews 10:36-39 and Hebrews 11:6.

    c) Fight the good fight of faith.
       1 Timothy 6:12.

4) Love

    a) Practice forbearance.
       Philippians 4:5.

    b) Pursue love.
       1 Timothy 6:11 and 2 Peter 1:7.

    c) Stay in the love of God.
       Jude 21.

5) Righteousness

    a) Live righteously.
       Titus 2:12.

    b) Pursue righteousness.
       1 Timothy 6:11.

    c) Stay active and do not grow weary in doing good.
       2 Thessalonians 3:6-13.

6) Discipline

    a) Practice self-control.
       2 Peter 1:6.

b) Pray in the Holy Spirit.
Jude 20.

c) Add knowledge of God's Word.
2 Timothy 3:14-17 and 2 Peter 1:5.

d) Be sound in judgment.
1 Peter 4:7.

e) Be sober in spirit.
1 Peter 4:7.

f) Pursue gentleness.
1 Timothy 6:11.

7) Worship

Continually offer up a sacrifice of praise to God.
Hebrews 13:15.

8) Hope

a) Be steadfast in hope.
1 Thessalonians 1:3.

b) Fix your hope on the revelation of Jesus.
1 Peter 1:13.

c) Hold fast to your confession of hope.
Hebrews 10:23.

9) Prophecy

a) Pay attention to prophecy.
2 Peter 1:19.

b) Look for the appearing of Jesus.
Titus 2:13.

c) Wait anxiously for the return of Jesus.
Jude 21 and Revelation 22:17.

B. Personal Attitudes

1) Put on the armor of light.
Romans 13:12.

    2)   Put on the breastplate of faith and love.
        1 Thessalonians 5:8.

    3)   Wear the helmet of the hope of salvation.
        1 Thessalonians 5:8.

    4)   Be confident of salvation.
        1 Timothy 6:12 and 2 Timothy 1:12.

    5)   Be zealous for good deeds.
        Titus 2:14.

    6)   Strengthen your heart.
        James 5:8.

    7)   Keep alert and sober in spirit.
        Mark 13:37; 1 Thessalonians 5:6; and 1 Peter 1:13.

    8)   Prepare your mind for action.
        1 Peter 1:13.

    9)   Rejoice in sufferings.
        1 Peter 4:13.

C. Conduct Toward Fellow Christians

    1)   Above all, abound in love toward one another.
        1 Thessalonians 3:12; 1 Peter 4:8; and 2 Peter 1:7.

    2)   Stimulate one another to love and good deeds.
        Hebrews 10:24.

    3)   Do not forsake assembling together.
        Hebrews 10:25.

    4)   Encourage one another.
        Hebrews 3:13 and Hebrews 10:25.

    5)   Do not complain against each other.
        James 5:9 and 1 Peter 4:9.

    6)   Be hospitable to one another.
        1 Peter 4:9.

    7)   Use spiritual gifts in serving one another.
        1 Peter 4:10.

8) Build up each other in faith.
    Jude 20.

9) Show mercy toward doubters.
    Jude 22.

D. Conduct Toward the World

1) Make no provision for the flesh.
    Romans 13:14.

    a) Deny worldly desires.
        Titus 2:12.

    b) Deny ungodliness.
        Titus 2:12.

    c) Abstain from carousing and drunkenness.
        Romans 13:13.

    d) Do not get involved in sexual promiscuity and sensuality.
        Romans 13:13.

    e) Avoid strife and jealousy.
        Romans 13:13.

    f) Flee from the love of money.
        1 Timothy 6:10-11.

    g) Be detached from worldly concerns and entanglements.
        1 Corinthians 7:29-32.

    h) Abstain from the passions of the flesh.
        1 Peter 2:11.

2) Save Souls.
    Jude 23.

E. Five Summary Passages

1) Romans 13:12-14. "The day is near," therefore:
    a) Lay aside deeds of darkness.
    b) Put on the armor of light.
    c) Behave properly.
    d) Don't get involved in carousing and drunkenness, sexual promiscuity and sensuality, or strife and jealousy.
    e) Put on the Lord Jesus Christ.
    f) Make no provision for the flesh.

2) 1 Timothy 6:10-15. "Until the appearing of our Lord Jesus Christ:"

    a) Flee from the love of money.
    b) Pursue righteousness, godliness, faith, love, perseverance and gentleness.
    c) Fight the good fight of faith.
    d) Take hold of the eternal life to which you were called.
    e) Keep the commandment without stain or reproach.

3) Titus 2:12-14. As we await the appearing of our "blessed hope:"

    a) Deny ungodliness and worldly desires.
    b) Live sensibly, righteously and godly.
    c) Look for the return of Jesus.
    d) Be zealous for good deeds.

4) 1 Peter 4:7-13. "The end of all things is near," therefore:

    a) Be of sound judgment.
    b) Be sober in spirit.
    c) Keep fervent in your love for one another.
    d) Be hospitable to one another.
    e) Do not complain against each other.
    f) Use spiritual gifts to serve each other.
    g) Rely on God's power to speak and serve.
    h) Be prepared for testing.
    i) Be ready to share in the sufferings of Christ.
    j) Keep on rejoicing.

5) 2 Peter. 1:5-11. Concerning "entrance into the eternal kingdom of our Lord and Savior Jesus Christ:"

    a) Begin with faith.
    b) Add virtue.
    c) Add knowledge.
    d) Add self-control.
    e) Add perseverance.
    f) Add godliness.
    g) Add brotherly kindness.
    h) Add love.

THE WOLF AND THE **LAMB** SHALL GRAZE TOGETHER, THE **LION** SHALL EAT STRAW LIKE THE OX, ... THEY SHALL DO **NO EVIL** OR HARM IN ALL MY HOLY MOUNTAIN, SAYS THE **LORD.** ISAIAH 65:25

The Midnight Cry

A song by Gary and Chuck Day ©

I hear the sound of a mighty rushing wind,
And it's closer now than it has ever been.
I can almost hear the trumpet
As Gabriel sounds the chord.
At the midnight cry, we'll be going home.

I look around me, I see prophecies fulfilled.
And the signs of the times,
They're appearing everywhere.
I can almost hear the Father as He says,
"Son, go get my children."
At the midnight cry, we'll be going home.

Refrain:
When Jesus steps out
On a cloud to call His children,
The dead in Christ shall rise
To meet Him in the air.
And then those that remain
Shall be quickly changed.
At the midnight cry
When Jesus comes again.

Maranatha!

Part Four

INDEXES OF
PROPHECIES

"And there are also many other
things which Jesus did, which if they
were written in detail, I suppose that
the world itself would not contain the
books that would be written." — John
21:25

Fingertips and Noses

A song by Eddie Carswell and Oliver Wells ©

Up in the hills somewhere in Kentucky
Is a little old school way back in the nothing
Where special kids born with special needs
Are sent to learn life's ABC's.

Their teacher, Mrs. Jones, tells them all about Jesus —
How in the twinkling of an eye He's coming back to get us,
About streets of gold and pearly gates.
And Oh! How they want to go, they just can't wait!
And she can't keep them in their seats.
They're all at the windows straining to see.

Chorus:
And it's fingertips and noses pressed to the window panes,
Longing eyes, expectant hearts for Him to come again.
All they know is that they love Him so,
And if He said He'd come, He's coming.
And they can't keep their windows clean
For fingerprints and noses.

She tried to explain to the kids about His coming.
She tried to calm them down, but they just wouldn't listen.
They just giggled and they clapped their hands.
They're so excited that He's coming for them,
And the first thing you know, they're out of their seats
Back at the windows straining to see.

Where will Jesus find us when He comes again?
Will we be like little children waiting just for Him,
With our fingertips and noses pressed to the window panes,
Longing eyes, expectant hearts for Him to come again?

A. Topical Index

B. Scripture Index

Other Prophecy Study Resources by Dr. Reagan
Available from Lamb & Lion Ministries

Books

God's Plan for the Ages — A comprehensive survey of all the major concepts and issues in Bible Prophecy. Easy to read and understand. This book has been published in many languages. 415 pages, $15.

Jesus is Coming Again! — A large format (8½ x 11") book about the end times for pre-school and elementary children. Beautifully illustrated throughout in full color. It is the only book ever published for children about end time prophecy. It focuses on the blessings that God has promised the world when Jesus returns. 28 pages, $7.

Living for Christ in the End Times — Tells how Christians can face up to and overcome the two greatest challenges to Christianity at the beginning of the 21st Century — namely, the decay of society and growing apostasy in the Church. Contains many insights about what the Bible says the world will be like in the end times, right before the return of Jesus. 264 pages, $10.

Wrath & Glory: The Meaning of Revelation — An interpretive overview of Revelation that is both readable and understandable. Answers the most commonly asked questions about the book and shows how it applies to Christian living. $10.

Audio Program

Revelation: An Overview— Twelve one hour tapes or CDs which will take you through the book of Revelation, verse by verse. Both the tapes and the CDs come in attractive albums. One of the ministry's most popular study resources. $35. Also available on one MP3 CD for $15.

Video Tapes

Preaching Bible Prophecy — An album containing two video tapes with four sermons about Bible prophecy. Taped live at Southeast Christian Church in Louisville, Kentucky. $25.

Israel in Bible Prophecy — A 65 minute video shot entirely in Israel. It focuses on seven prophecies being fulfilled in Israel today that point to the soon return of Jesus. $18.

The Rapture Kit — A multi-media study of the Rapture. The album contains a video tape, a cassette tape, and a teacher's manual. There are four 25 minute video programs. The cassette tape contains six audio segments. These materials can be combined to present a total of seven in-depth lessons on all aspects of the Rapture. The teacher's manual contains study outlines for students. $35.

The Signs of the Times Kit — A multi-media kit similar to the one about the Rapture. It contains four video programs and three audio segments which can be combined to produce seven lessons on the signs of the times. Also like the Rapture Kit, it contains a teacher's manual with study outlines that can be reproduced for students. $35.

To order any of the above items, call **1-800-705-8316.** There will be a nominal shipping charge. For Texas residents, there will also be a state sales tax.

Call the same number to get a copy of the ministry's tape and publications catalogue or to subscribe (free of charge) to the ministry's bi-monthly prophecy magazine called the *Lamplighter.*